Praise for *There's No Such Thing As 'Naughty'*

'As a parenting support book [*There's No Such Thing As 'Naughty'*] is in a class of its own in terms of the accessible wisdom and pragmatic help it provides. It is perhaps the most helpful book for parents of children of any age. Written by a great communicator, it will have massive impact'
Professor Peter Fonagy, CEO Anna Freud National Centre for Children & Families

'Kate has devoted much of her emotional as well as her academic mind to develop her approach to being a nurturing and loving parent. This book reflects Kate's genuine passion about children's mental well-being'
Dame Benny Refson DBE, President Place2Be

'We know that a child's early experiences play a vital role in supporting healthy brain growth, which is key to their future mental and physical well-being. This book provides a fun, accessible introduction to developmental neuroscience that can help parents and carers support their child's brain development'
Sir Peter Wanless, Chief Executive NSPCC

'Kate writes with humour and compassion, and without judgement, turning a potentially daunting subject into a personal one'
Susan Cooke, Head of Research and Evidence NSPCC

About the author

In 25 years as a journalist, Kate Silverton has become one of the BBC's leading and most popular broadcasters. She has produced and presented numerous documentaries, including for the BBC's flagship current-affairs programme *Panorama*. She has come under fire on the frontline in Iraq and Afghanistan, covered the glamour of the Oscars in Hollywood, and stepped out beneath the glitter ball herself as a contestant for the BBC's much-loved entertainment show, *Strictly Come Dancing*. Kate has spent decades interviewing leading figures throughout the world, from politicians through to celebrities and scientists.

Throughout it all, Kate's lifelong passion has been to advocate for children and their emotional well-being. Her academic roots are in child development with a BSc in psychology and, after having children of her own, Kate decided to retrain as a child psychotherapist. She now combines her career in journalism with her studies, currently volunteering as a counsellor on placement working with children at a London primary school. Philanthropically, for many years she has supported charities like Place2Be, the Anna Freud National Centre for Children and Families, The South London and Maudsley NHS Foundation Trust, as well as the NSPCC and the Duke and Duchess of Cambridge's Royal Foundation. Kate's counselling work with children, her own personal experience of psychotherapy and the interviews she has conducted with world-renowned psychiatrists, neuroscientists and psychotherapists have all informed her approach and the concept she has devised for this book. Her philosophy is, 'If we get it right from conception to five, we can set our children up for life.' Her passion is to share what she has learned with as many parents as she can, to help them to have the parenting experience they always hoped to have, and for their children to have the parenting experience they deserve.

Kate lives in London with her husband Mike, daughter Clemency, nine, son Wilbur, six, and their dog, a black working cocker spaniel named Gatsby.

KATE SILVERTON

there's no such thing as 'naughty'

The groundbreaking guide for parents with children aged 0–5

PIATKUS

PIATKUS

First published in Great Britain in 2021 by Piatkus

5 7 9 10 8 6 4

A CIP catalogue record for this book
is available from the British Library.

ISBN 978-0-349-42852-9

Typeset in Goudy by M Rules
Printed and bound in Great Britain by Clays Ltd, Elcograf S.p.A.

Papers used by Piatkus are from well-managed forests
and other responsible sources.

Piatkus
An imprint of
Little, Brown Book Group
Carmelite House
50 Victoria Embankment
London EC4Y 0DZ

An Hachette UK Company
www.hachette.co.uk

www.littlebrown.co.uk

NOTE: the names of some individuals featured in this book
have been changed to protect their privacy.

To Mike, Clemency and Wilbur,
to my sea and my stars.

Contents

I dedicate this book to all parents, everywhere. I pay tribute to those of you who are parenting as a team, those who are parenting solo, those of you who are bereaved, divorced or separated, those of you who are grandparents, foster carers, step-parents, adoptive parents and primary carers – all of you who are the wonderful, empathic, kind, caring people who have taken on the role of raising a child – very often the most challenging job in the world . . . unquestionably the most important.

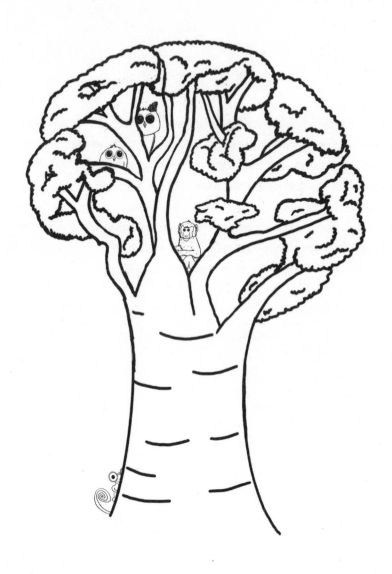

This is the story of three animals and a tree: the lizard, the baboon, the wise owl and the baobab, and how together they represent our brain, and how they each influence our children's – and indeed our own – behaviour.

It's a story that explains why, for our children under five, there really is no such thing as 'naughty'.

And why, if we get it right from conception to five, we can set our children up for life.

I am so excited to be able to show you how.

Introduction –
Why I Wrote This Book

When I finally became a mother, after many years of heartache, with four failed IVFs, two miscarriages and total emotional exhaustion, I was overjoyed! I had fallen pregnant naturally, at the age of 40, which seemed amazing given that even the doctors seemed to have given up hope; then, at 43, I conceived naturally again. My children, Clemency and Wilbur, honestly felt like gifts from the universe. There was the obvious elation and absolute gratitude, but it was accompanied by many questions, too:

Firstly, *wow* – why did no one tell us it would be this tough?
Secondly, erm . . . why *was* it so tough?!
and thirdly . . . is everyone else finding it this tough?!

Six weeks into welcoming Clemency home, even my former Royal Marines commando husband exclaimed, 'Getting my green beret was easier than this!' Followed up later with, 'I had more advice when getting a puppy!'

It's true, the tougher realities of parenting are rarely shared between friends; my husband jokes we'd probably never do it otherwise! I think it's perhaps because we're increasingly parenting in isolation, without the support of the more traditional community that we would once have been a part of. We could parent more by instinct then, when we weren't so sleep-deprived and had the benefit of an extended family to help cook and be with baby, while elders passed down ancient wisdoms from generation to generation.

We may live in different times but we all still have the same hopes and aspirations, the same dream of being the best parents we can be, to want the reassurance that we are 'getting it right' and to know that our children are growing up feeling valued, safe and loved.

And, clearly, we **do** get advice, but in recent decades it seems some of it has been designed more with frazzled parents in mind (understandably, absolutely) rather than what might necessarily work best *for our children*. For example, we have seen the advent of the 'naughty step' and 'banishing to rooms', or even leaving our children to 'cry it out' alone. All done with the best of intentions, to help time-poor parents just trying to stay afloat. But what if we could combine the *best* of our ancient wisdoms, *backed up* by modern science in a way that not only benefited us . . . but benefited our children, too?

Faced with a children's mental health crisis, we want, more than ever, to feel confident we are raising compassionate, considerate, kind children; children who become adults who are emotional adventurers, able to overcome adversity and embrace life in all its glorious multi-colour.

Once I had become a mother, I was keen to learn more about how I could best support my own children's mental well-being, as much as their physical health, too.

As a journalist, I have been fortunate to have access to some of the world's most brilliant clinical psychoanalysts like Professor Peter Fonagy, neuroscientists and psychiatrists such as Dr Bruce Perry, and clinicians and psychotherapists, Dr Gabor Maté, Dr Margot Sunderland and psychotherapist Liza Elle. I invited child psychiatrists into my kitchen for a cup of tea . . . and asked them to 'bring their brain' (as you do), but I meant it literally. I had read so many parenting books and looked at so many different theories – and encountered quite a few myths along the way – that I wanted to hear *them* explain why our children behave the way they do and, most importantly, how we, as parents, might best respond.

I wanted to learn how to parent a healthy brain.

I knew, from my training as a children's counsellor and my own experience of psychotherapy, that what we experience when we are very young shapes the adult we become. What I had *not* known, and what *blew me away*, was when I learned that what happens in our childhood can impact EVERYTHING, from our brain development, to our biology, *as well as* our behaviour. How we, as parents, respond to our children's behaviour will directly influence their brain development.

I suddenly saw my children in a totally different light – or rather, I saw their *behaviour* in a totally different light. I discovered I could tackle tantrums and meltdowns with ease, solve squabbles in seconds and saw how sibling rivalry has its roots in fear. I found parenting SO much easier – and my children were happier, too! With everything I was learning, I felt able to parent more confidently and intuitively, rather than feeling I was in the dark. It was an ABSOLUTE REVELATION. And to my husband, brought up in a 'spare the rod, spoil the child' environment, the approach we began to use was transformational for him, too.

And all without a 'naughty step' in sight!

I have written this book to share what I have learned, because it seems too important not to. I think EVERY parent deserves to know the secret to raising emotionally healthy children. Not only does it serve our children well for the future, but it makes our lives EASIER and an awful lot more FUN!

I wanted to share **the secret to parenting a healthy brain.**

It is something scientists have known for decades. However, what they have known (and to be fair, wanted us to know, too) has not really reached the parenting mainstream.

Why?

Because – as they told me when I asked them that question – 'science likes labels' and 'science does "complicated"'. Professor Fonagy challenged me to, 'explain it as a story, to keep it simple'.

And so that's what I set out to do.

I took the liberty of renaming the (very complicated) structure of the brain and came up with a (*very* simple) concept to explain how our children's developing brains influence their behaviour.

The concept involves just three animals and a tree: the lizard, the baboon, the wise owl and the baobab. It's SUPER-EASY to explain and SUPER-EASY to put into practice.

I wanted a concept that was simple to understand, even for our children, and that we as parents can put to use in seconds – even, and when, we're under significant parental duress!

It is important for me to emphasise that there *is* science in this here book! I say that because I want you to feel empowered by it. I have written about it in a way that is really accessible, because I am passionate that EVERY parent should have access to it. Because with the science in your sails, as it were, you can be confident to move forward, trusting your instincts, using the concept of the lizard, baboon and wise owl, knowing that what you are doing for your children is *supported by hard science.*

You'll also find what I call 'Brain Boxes' scattered throughout the book, which include elements of the research I have done, the clinical studies I have read, and the analysis and knowledge of the people I have interviewed and been inspired by. There are plenty of resources and support networks at the back of the book, too, if you want to delve even deeper. At all times, though – and I can't stress this enough – the language is simple and the concept easy to use.

Part I

The first two chapters set out the stall, as it were. They will explain how your parenting shapes the person your child becomes: their attitudes to risk, their resilience, even their future relationships. It's THAT important for you to know! It will explain your child's behaviour using the concept of the three animals and the baobab tree so that by the end of the very *first* chapter, you'll be **ready** and equipped with all that you need to know to be an all-knowing neuroscience ninja ready to tackle every and all types of behaviour – from tantrums and tears through to fights and fears. I swear, cross my heart, you totally will. So stay with me here . . . that parenting ninja badge has your name on it!

Part II

I explore all those universal parenting scenarios ... you know, the ones we all dread: the public meltdowns, the angry outbursts, the 'refusals to soldier' (as my husband Mike puts it), as well as many others too, including coping with starting nursery or school, with bereavement, separation or divorce. I will also share many scenarios from personal experience – not sparing myself any embarrassment either – to ensure you know you really are not alone. You'll also hear from other parents who share their experience, including my husband, which is important as in his case he originally came at this with a somewhat different perspective!

In every chapter you'll find easy and practical tips and tools to use, as well as some scripts to follow too, because I know that when we are at the end of our parenting tether, we often just want someone to show us HOW! And NOW!

Parenting can be tough. We may often be operating alone, and running on empty. I am a working mum who came late to motherhood. I know how exhausting it can be. I know, having young children of my own, the difficulties that modern parenthood can pose. I now understand why raising children has been described as the toughest job in the world.

However, I also understand, with everything I have learned in the past decade, that we are far more powerful than we know, more capable than we might believe and certainly we all have the ability to raise children who are healthy and happy and can share the strongest bond with us for life.

My hope is that this book will help enable you to be the parent you always hoped and wanted to be. I hope it will help you feel supported to enjoy your *own* journey, feeling nurtured and empowered throughout and, most of all, to help your little one to thrive with a childhood that is rich in happiness and fun. I hope this helps us all to build a better future for our children, and for us all to have a wonderful time while we do.

Shall we begin? Let's dive in, I am with you all the way.

Kate Silverton, February 2021

PART I

Understanding Your Child – the Lizard, the Baboon and the Wise Owl Way

I believe we are best served as parents when we are able to step inside the minds of our children, to really understand how they think and what drives their behaviour. It's so much easier to do that when we understand how their brains develop. Part I is going to explain your child's brain using the super-simplistic concept of just three animals: a lizard, a baboon and a wise old owl! I look at it this way, the brain may be complex but our understanding of it doesn't have to be.

With this newfound knowledge, you'll understand *everything* about your children's behaviour and why there really is no such thing as 'naughty'!

CHAPTER 1

The Lizard, the Baboon
and the Wise Owl

'See a child differently – see a different child.'

DR STUART G. SHANKER, professor emeritus of
philosophy and psychology at York University

'She's going through the terrible twos!'

'My baby's so clingy.'

'My daughter can't share.'

'My son's a biter.'

'My twins won't sit still!'

'Why can't we leave the house on time?!'

'My daughter's so ANGRY – she keeps hitting her sister.'

'WHY won't they just DO AS THEY'RE TOLD?!'

Why DO our children behave the way they do?

Old-school parenting might say our children are 'NAUGHTY'.

I say old-school parenting is wrong!

Our children are *not* 'naughty' – *they're just trying to tell us something.* In the only way they know how.

Our children under five will often 'act out' their feelings because they don't always have the words to *explain* them just yet. And their feelings can seem MASSIVE, like the WHOLE WORLD is about to end, because they don't have an advanced 'emotional filter' at this age, no means of switching themselves off or turning down the dial. When we understand that, when we are able to interpret their behaviour easily (which you'll be able to do by the end of this chapter!), you'll see why I say, 'THERE'S NO SUCH THING AS NAUGHTY' and we become parents who can ask not 'What is WRONG with you?', but rather, 'What's going on for you right now that I need to help you with?'

That's it!

I know it sounds simple, but helping your children to learn how to manage their big feelings will be one of the biggest and BEST investments you will EVER make as a parent. There really is no need for you to feel pressured to create a little Einstein or Mozart. If we want rounded, grounded, happy kids, science confirms what

Nature already knew: teaching our children how to handle their emotions is vital for ensuring their future mental and emotional well-being. The beauty of it is, Nature has already given us everything we need to help them do it.

'Rather than hold up flashcards to a baby, it would be more appropriate to the baby's stage of development to simply hold him and enjoy him.'

Psychotherapist Sue Gerhardt in her book, *Why Love Matters*

Our emotions are the feelings we sense inside us. They are our guide to what is safe in life and what is not, what we move towards and what we run away from.

How our children experience the world, and our role as parents, will shape the person they become; not only their physical health, but in their mental and emotional well-being, too. We can help them best when we understand that our children's brains are <u>still</u> developing, which means they might behave and perceive things very differently from the way we do.

By way of illustration, when you look at this, what do you see?

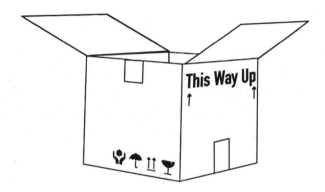

Well, here's what your child sees . . .

ROCKET SHIP?! RACE CAR?!

FORT?! MANSION?!

Our children at this age experience the world differently – because *their brains are different*. Their brains are engaged in growing, in exploring, in learning. That's because our children's brains are not yet as developed as ours. In fact, the work of Professor Peter Fonagy, and many researchers in this field, suggests that the human brain does not stop developing until we are around 25, so your child under five has a brain that is still VERY much a work in progress, which means that their behaviour will be, too.

As soon as I learned about brain development, everything about my young children suddenly made sense, from why they found it difficult to share, why my son was hitting his sister and why we all found it so bloody hard to get out of the door on time!

I could avert tantrums and embrace tears, stop the fighting and see my children become firm friends without resorting to 'old-school' punishments like 'naughty steps' or 'banishment' to bedrooms. I found I could be the parent I wanted to be, with an ability to 'step inside my children's heads', to see things from their perspective and to understand what it was they were feeling and, most importantly, WHY.

Understanding how our children's brains develop is absolutely vital if we are to help them – and indeed ourselves! – to navigate the rest of life happily, whatever the challenge.

However, the brain is a complex organ and I am a bear with a rather small brain when it comes to neuroscience. When I set out to learn about the brain, all the talk of amygdalas, limbic systems and dorsal vagus nerves conjured up images of computer-coding courses or a German car advert more than the incredible organ that keeps us alive.

So, I set out to distil the science, to create a very simple concept that helped me to understand my children's behaviour in a way that made sense to me – and in a way, I hope, that will make sense to you, too. Because it is my dearest wish that in sharing it with you, you'll see why 'THERE IS NO SUCH THING AS NAUGHTY' and, by the end of this chapter, you'll be the one explaining to your friends why!

The lizard, the baboon and the wise owl

When our ancestors began to walk on two legs, they could naturally use their hands more freely and scientists believe the increase in intelligence as a result of being able to do more activities led to a dramatic increase in brain size. However, standing on two legs had another consequence, too.

'At the same time, standing on two legs produced a narrowed pelvis and birth canal in females. The bigger head and smaller pelvis meant the human infant had to be born very immature.'

Dr Margot Sunderland, Director of Education and Training, Centre for Child Mental Health, London, in her book, *The Science of Parenting*.

Having a relatively 'unfinished brain' means we are far more vulnerable at birth and for a significantly longer period than our mammalian cousins; for example, zebras can run from predators only an hour after birth; a baby giraffe will drop six feet from its mother's womb and walk, albeit quite wobbly, almost immediately after; dolphins are *born* swimming. In stark contrast, our babies are born pretty much helpless. It takes around a year for children to start walking with confidence, and they cannot feed or care for themselves for even longer.

Our children are completely dependent upon us for their survival, until their immature brains effectively 'catch up'. It's why there is such rapid brain growth in the first few years of life: our children's brains have to work *quickly* to achieve the skills and abilities they need to survive and flourish in whatever environment they find themselves in.

Now the brain develops in a hierarchical fashion – from bottom to top, as it were. To allow it to be more easily understood, scientists have typically divided it into parts. All the parts are present from birth and each is connected to the other, but each part has its own distinct functions, too.

To understand our children and why they do what they do, we must first understand these different parts and how they influence our children's behaviour.

The first parts of our children's brains to develop are what are known as the brain stem and cerebellum – what we think of as our SURVIVAL BRAIN. As the name implies, its job is to keep our children alive. It governs heart rate and body temperature, our children's sleep patterns, their breathing, balance, appetite and digestion. The survival brain responds to anything that's potentially life-threatening – whether that's something happening inside the body, for example if our children are hungry – or externally, for example someone is running towards them waving their fists and shouting.

In these circumstances, our children's survival brain acts instinctively and automatically. Its responses are not consciously chosen and involve what we understand to be our fight–flight and freeze responses. The survival brain is what our babies are mostly dependent upon in the womb, and it will drive a lot of their behaviour during the first year of life.

Next we have the limbic brain, or what is also known as the EMOTIONAL BRAIN. It's involved in processing and regulating our children's 'big feelings', like anger and joy, as well as their social behaviour; how they relate to other people. It's also how our babies and young children will process what's going on in the world around them – what they see, hear, taste, smell and touch. It's where much of their memory and language is 'located' as well as their stress response – how they **act** if they sense they are in danger.

The survival and emotional parts of our brains are often referred to as our 'lower brain' and are very much interconnected.

Finally, we come to the cortex, specifically the pre-frontal cortex or the THINKING BRAIN. Also referred to as our HIGHER brain, it is the part of the brain that sets us apart from other animals. It helps our children to learn, to have empathy (to think about things from someone else's perspective), to think about the past and the future, to problem solve and to understand 'concepts'.

ALL the parts of the brain ARE present from birth, but because each part develops in 'sequence', as it were, with the brain stem first, and the thinking brain last, some parts can be more influential than others in terms of our children's behaviour in their early years.

So, as I have said, I love the brain – it's brilliant – but I can get awfully lost in labels like cerebellum and hypothalamus! I could take up pages here explaining each and every one of the brain's intricate functions (don't worry, I won't), and I think the complexity of the labelling is one of the main reasons the invaluable research carried out in recent decades has not reached an even wider audience. However, what we now know about our children's brain development, especially in the early years, is fundamental for their future mental health and well-being and can help us enormously with our parenting, too. So, I challenged myself to distil decades of science into one simple concept in the hope that it will go some way to helping us understand our children's behaviour a little better.

It involves . . . wait for it . . .

A tree, a lizard, a baboon and a wise owl (I know . . . you're very welcome ☺ 🙊).

Remember, this is my interpretation – and, of course, your child DOESN'T ACTUALLY have a lizard, baboon or wise owl in their head, but I find using imagery is a really helpful way to explain what I have understood from all the research and interviews I have carried out.

Clearly I would still really love for you to take a deep dive into the incredible neuroscience and the pioneering work of scientists like Professor Peter Fonagy, Dr Bruce Perry and Dr Margot Sunderland and many others referenced in this book, who have influenced me throughout my studies (I reference them in full at the back of the book), However, moving forward, we can now bin 'bilateral integration' and cast aside 'Mr Cerebellum' and, with some fanfare, I now introduce you to your child's brain (and yours by the way!) using just three animals and a tree.

And not just any old tree, but an incredible ancient baobab tree from my beloved Zimbabwe. Known there as the tree of wisdom, it is the tree around which the elders would gather t o pass down generations of knowledge to the young children of the village.

We are going to take the baobab tree as a whole to represent our children's brain. At the bottom of the trunk there's a little lizard sitting on the bark. The lizard represents our SURVIVAL BRAIN. I think of it as a lizard because this part of our brains is – remarkably – the same brain that reptiles also have and, indeed, have had for hundreds of millions of years! It is very primitive but, as we have seen, it plays a vital role in keeping us safe and alive.

The lizard

Imagine a lizard in the wild. It acts on instinct. If it's hungry and a fly buzzes past, its tongue shoots out and that's it, lunch done. If it hears a rustle in the long grass nearby, it will be up and off in an instant, or it might stand stock still, hoping to blend into the background and avoid detection. Well, it's the same for us: our lizard brain is there for our survival and will react in a flash, whether it's when we are hungry or thirsty, too hot or too cold, or if it thinks we are about to be attacked.

Our lizard is involved in what is known as our 'stress response'. The symptoms of fear first arise here in the brain stem and it can see us in fight–flight–freeze mode – that is to say if we feel threatened we may stand our ground and fight, or we might turn and flee, just like the lizard, or in the same way, if there appears little chance of escape we might simply freeze . . . hoping the threat will disappear.

The lizard does not 'choose' to behave in a certain way – its behaviour is automatic. We can see it in reality with our own children's 'quick-as-a-flash' behaviour; for example, meltdowns in public when our child might drop like a dead weight to the floor – suggesting their 'lizard' has become completely overwhelmed by what they are experiencing in much the same way we adults might faint or freeze if we too are 'overcome' by a particularly stressful situation.

It's the lizard brain in play when our baby's body stiffens if she's startled, or if she is frightened by a loud noise and she's on her back, her arms and legs might flail as though trying to run away. If your baby howled the bathroom down when you gave him his first bath, you might imagine the lizard leaping to his defence in protest at the shock of the sudden change in temperature. And it's the lizard who drives that most urgent of cries as our baby tells us in no uncertain terms, 'I'M HUNGRY!'

The lizard is not sophisticated or manipulative – it doesn't sit there rubbing its little claws thinking: *Mmmm . . . I'm going to make the baby scream and scream because I know it p*sses Mum and Dad off!*

Noooo! Absolutely not. The lizard's only job is to ensure your child's survival. It acts automatically, alerting you to what your children need *precisely* when they need it. How you respond is key, because here's the thing: the LIZARD's healthy development is crucial, not only for your child's <u>physical health</u> but for their future <u>mental health</u> too.

Because how the lizard develops can help shape our children's future behaviour and their attitudes towards things like risk, their tendency towards anxiety and how fearful they are, both as children and the adult they become. And the lizard's development and the associations it makes (whether the world is a scary place or a welcoming one), begins REALLY EARLY.

> **Brain Box** 'Brain building begins just two weeks after conception. And from conception, we all have two core needs: **stable, caring relationships and enriching experiences.** These two core needs are critical elements of the environment in which we develop – and they are just as important for positive development as food and safety.'
>
> Professor Peter Fonagy, Anna Freud Centre for Children and Families

I was blown away when I first understood that the experiences we have within the womb and in our first year of life will directly shape the adult we become. It's why my wonderful midwife, the eminent Jenny Smith, says everyone needs to know it. 'It is at the point of conception that we need to empower women with the knowledge that even at the earliest weeks of pregnancy they are supporting and influencing not just the growth of their baby physically but that of the development of their baby's brain. This development starts in the womb then continues into childhood, and these influences impact the adult your child becomes.'

With so many new experiences in their first year of life, it can feel pretty scary for our babies, especially when we consider that they are literally trapped inside their bodies, helpless, unable to run away from threat or feed themselves when they are hungry. In large part, the lizard initially depends entirely upon us for its survival. When you hold your baby (or your young child), when you keep her close, keeping her warm and feeling safe, so you are helping to 'reassure' that ancient part of her brain – our meta-phorical lizard – that when she is hungry, thirsty, frightened or in pain, you will be there to help, to keep her safe – to keep her alive.

Every time you respond to your baby when she calls for you, every time you soothe and comfort her and provide for her needs, you are helping to build up positive associations in your baby's brain.

Brain Box

'Being able to feel safe with other people is probably the single most important aspect of mental health; safe connections are fundamental to meaningful and satisfying lives.'

Bessel A. van der Kolk, psychiatrist, researcher and author of *The Body Keeps the Score: Brain, Mind and Body in the Healing of Trauma*

The more positive associations that your child's 'lizard' makes (namely, that if/when he needs you, you'll be there), the more likely your child is to be able to cope with challenges in the future. Consider how we help our children to first learn to ride a bicycle. We don't just shove them off to cycle alone on the first time of trying. We initially act as their stabilisers, steadying them as they find their balance, helping them to practice until they can go it alone. After a while, we stand back, cheering from the sidelines, still there to kiss a grazed knee if they fall. In a similar way, having us there as a 'stabiliser' at the start of their life journey enables our children to gain the confidence to 'find their balance', to try new things and ultimately, of course, to go it alone.

This is how the roots of resilience are grown. Resilience is borne not from 'throwing our young children in at the deep end' but rather first laying strong foundations, providing unconditional love and support, in this initial, most vulnerable period of their lives. In doing this now, we are helping our children to build strong healthy foundations in the brain that will last them a lifetime.

In conclusion then:

1.   Our children's lizard 'brain' is what keeps them alive.
2.   It doesn't CHOOSE to act the way it does . . . it acts instinctively, and automatically, alerting you to their needs.
3.   It remains a huge influence on our children, particularly in their earliest years, but throughout their entire lives too.
4.   It plays a part in our children's attitudes to risk, their tendency towards anxiety and their future mental health.

So what about the rest of the brain?

Well, let's look at our baobab brain again, and there, higher up on one of its branches, is a . . .

BABOON

The baboon in my concept rep-resents the EMOTIONAL BRAIN or what scientists call the limbic system. It's the same brain as other mammals, like your dog or cat. The baboon is in charge of our children's social behaviour, such as care and nurturing, playfulness and bonding. He's in charge of all the big emotions like fear and rage, joy and trust. Your child's 'baboon' cannot register concepts like time (he doesn't wear a watch!), nor can he apply logic; he's a baboon and lives very much in the here and now. The baboon, like the lizard, is responsible for our children's safety and survival. I think of him as a self-defence system, watchful and alert. I imagine him, sat on the branch of the baobab tree, scanning the horizon for any potential threat. If he sees anything untoward, he might leap down to the ground, beating his chest to ward off anyone he doesn't want to get too close. Our children's baboons take their cues from other people's body language, their eyes especially, the same way as other mammals like dogs do. The baboon helps our children to form good relationships, to become attached to others – another survival mechanism when you consider it, because there is more security in being part of a wider 'troop' or tribe.

The baboon really comes into his own during our children's first three years of life and, as we will see, it's why our toddler's behaviour might sometimes seem much more akin to a cheeky baboon than a human being! (With a little boy who is now six, what do you think inspired me?!) All that throwing themselves around, snatching food or toys, beating their fists on the floor – behaviour we might consider just a tad 'over the top'!

Being able to think of our children as more primitive creatures, driven by a 'lizard' and 'baboon' whose focus is more about staying alive and less about the 'please and thank-yous', can help us to keep perspective in those moments of meltdowns and angry outbursts. When we remember that our children's behaviour is driven by a still-developing brain, we may be more accepting when they don't always behave the way we want or expect them to.

When we can understand what's driving our child's behaviour, when we soothe, support and reassure them if they feel threatened or afraid, it helps to build positive associations in the brain and strengthen loving bonds between us. It leads to what we refer to in psychotherapy as having a 'secure attachment'. The British psychiatrist John Bowlby defined attachment as a 'lasting psychological connectedness between human beings'. It means when our children are under stress, feel threatened or afraid, they will readily call or come to us because they have learned we can help them, that they can trust us to allay their fears and contain their big feelings. Having secure attachment helps to support our children's future emotional and mental well-being. It influences everything from how they handle stress in later life to their future relationships – yes, even the romantic ones!

Brain Box

'There is strong evidence from neuroscience that supports attachment theory and suggests that 0–5 years is a critical period for developing attachment. If no attachment relationship at all has developed during this period, then the child is likely to have learning, health, or social issues, as we see in children brought up in very emotionally deprived circumstances. One way attachment can be strengthened is through serve and return interactions between 0–5s and their parents, caregivers and others. Like a rally in a game of tennis, babies and very young children naturally reach out for interaction with adults through babbling, pointing, imitating facial expressions and so on. This process drives the development of important language, cognitive, and social skills and is one of the key ingredients that builds a child's brain.'

Professor Peter Fonagy, Anna Freud Centre for Children and Families

As Professor Fonagy also explains, 'A strong foundation in the early years increases the chances of positive health and learning later on, while a weak foundation increases the odds of later difficulties.' How we interact with our children now is that important.

In this book, we'll look at LOTS of examples of baboon behaviour (snatching, hitting, and the ultimate meltdowns) and how we might best respond, to get the best 'game of tennis' with our children that we can! I'll share the tips, tools and tricks to allow you to work with your children in their more challenging moments, to quickly bring your young baboons back 'down to earth' without too many tears or throwing themselves around! With a clear understanding and insight into our children's brain development (and indeed our own), we can more easily interpret their behaviour as not 'naughty' per se, but as behaviour that's a consequence of them having a still-developing baboon brain.

Our little baboons will often act first and think later, especially if they feel threatened – perhaps if another toddler snatches their favourite toy, a sibling grabs *their* piece of cake, or another child becomes too physical during play at nursery, etc. It's at these times that our baboons might lash out in response if they have not yet learned how to control their impulsive behaviour.

We can help our children to manage their emotions – or what we call self-regulate – by helping them to *recognise* the emotions they feel inside. Dr Allan Schore is one of the leading clinical psychologists of his generation, and he maintains that encouraging emotional regulation is one of the most fundamental things we parents can do for our very young children.

> **Brain Box** 'The key development of children happens in the first two years of life – the developing brain doubles in size in the first year and in the second year particularly numerous delicate nerve connections form patterns in the brain. They will form regardless – the question is whether they will be healthy and stabilising patterns or not. Crucially the parts of the brain which control emotional stability, self-control and conscience form early.'
>
> Dr Allan Schore, 2013

If it all sounds a little far-fetched, think about the adults you know who STILL use their baboon rather too often. Consider the man (or woman!) who 'throws their toys out of the pram' at work, or the driver who snarls with road rage, waving their fists and shouting at other motorists with indignant anger ... all baboons in action.

There is the fun baboon stuff, too: the social bonding, the playfulness, the curiosity and verbal communication, the ability to care for and nurture others, and what I think of as a memory sack that helps our children to house their experiences and the emotions that give colour and texture to them.

The baboon helps our children to record their memories, the good ones as well as the not-so-great ones, in what essentially we might think of as a 'library of experiences'. Every day, your child's baboon will add to the list of experiences: what is fun to do and what is not, what is safe to do without you present and what isn't.

When our children ask us for a pillow fight or a wrestle, when they clamber on the climbing frame, this is all behaviour driven by their baboon, urging them to be curious and playful, building up fun memories to store in that wonderful memory sack.

As they gain in confidence, your child's baboon will be urging them to try out new things, to gain some independence. It is testament to your brilliance as a parent when they do, because it means they trust you to be there for them if they fail!

And an important point to note in this regard, if our children seem selfish and demanding and 'all about me' at times during these early years, it's because they are designed by evolution to be that way. It's all about survival, remember!

* * *

If we dismiss our children's behaviour as going through the 'terrible twos', label them as 'naughty' or accuse them of being 'drama queens', we are really missing the point: at this age, their brains are very much a work in progress and there simply isn't as much rational thinking going on as there is in ours.

The good news is, we can work with our children to help their lizard and baboon develop healthily and, in doing so, we will reduce their more extreme behaviour over time.

How do we do this?

Ahhhh, well, here's where we come to our 'thinking brain', or what we will from now on call . . .

The Wise Owl

The wise owl represents our 'higher or thinking brain', specifically the pre-frontal cortex. It is the most developed part of the brain and its sophistication is what sets us apart from other animals. It gives us powers of reasoning and imagination, and the ability to problem solve. That's why I think of this part of our brain as a wise owl, sitting amid the canopy of leaves and branches at the very top of our brain – the 'baobab tree'.

The wise owl is in charge of all the wonderfully complex thoughts we have. She understands concepts such as time and conscience, she can analyse, story-tell, rationalise, be creative, manage strong feelings, reason, show kindness, logic, empathy and concern – even generate abstract thought and imagination. The wise owl allows us to take a 'big picture view'. Sitting there high up in the tree, she has perspective and so she can put situations into context. If a stranger approaches on the horizon, our lizard and baboon might become jumpy and restless, ready to attack or run if need be. The wise owl, from her lofty position, can see whether the stranger is friend or foe and can decide with the benefit of her 'big picture view' how best to respond. She brings calm and can regulate the more primitive behaviours of our baboon and lizard. She understands that sometimes they HAVE to act the way they do – in order to keep us alive – but she also knows when she's needed to swoop down from her branch and scoop the lizard and baboon up in her broad, feathered wings to calm and soothe them if they need her to, or perhaps she might work with them as a team to deal with any potential threat together.

Our wise owl brain is what allows us to distinguish right from wrong or what we might consider to be 'ethical judgements' along with many other skills that enable us to live harmoniously in society.

As adults, *the wise owl is crucial for our own emotional self-regulation* – our ability to soothe ourselves and our emotions, and to trust that we can respond to any situation, however challenging, in a considered and confident way.

But . . . breaking news – here's the headline!

OUR YOUNG CHILDREN DON'T HAVE A WISE OWL YET!

Nope, NADA, nuh-uh . . .

WHAT THEY HAVE IS MORE FLUFFY OWLET THAN WISE OWL – it's an owlet who can't even fly just yet. She has little wings which means she can't swoop down and scoop the lizard and baboon up to comfort them. She's not able to help to quickly calm them down when they need her to.

The owlet needs time to grow, to become the all-wise owl that we adults are. Our gorgeous small people are only just starting out on life's incredible voyage of discovery. In these first few years of life, their brains are very much running to catch up. And even then, it's still very much a work in progress.

So far in their lives, our children's ancient brains have been all-consumed by their survival, not how to get out of the house on time or whether or not it is appropriate to have a meltdown in the supermarket; their focus has been on gaining some all-important independence so that they have a better chance of staying alive if ever abandoned out on the 'savannah'!

Understanding the concept of time or having consciousness to resolve a moral dilemma or knowing right from wrong are, frankly, at this point surplus to requirements! So, m'lud, we cannot find our children guilty of being 'naughty' when their brains are still developing.

Our children cannot easily 'contain' their big feelings in these early years. We have to help them in order for them to be able to do it themselves. We have to help them grow that fluffy owlet into a beautiful wise owl.

* * *

However, parenting is not always easy, as we know. When we ourselves are tired or afraid, our own lizards and baboons are more likely to leap into action before *our* wise owl has even had a chance to swoop in to help. Again, looking at it from an evolutionary perspective, we might understand why our baboon is more on guard if we are 'compromised' in any way, whether we're tired or if we are stressed and on edge.

As parents, this knowledge and insight about how our own brains function can help us to become more self-aware, to ensure we remain connected to our own wise owl, rather than operating first and foremost from our lizard and baboon, especially when we're juggling emails, wiping bottoms and wondering why we're yelling when our four-year-olds are running riot.

Let's take a real-life example. When my son Wilbur started school, aged four, we proudly bought his uniform, including a packet of white-collared polo shirts. He happily wore one on the first day, but on the second, he refused, flat out. 'I'll wear *this* one,' he said, pulling out a blue T-shirt, 'but *not* this one'. But that one wasn't part of his uniform! Battle commenced, with me using every tactic I could muster to get my son to pull the white polo shirt over his head and get to school on time. With five minutes to go, he was still parked on the stairs, face red, tears streaming. The school gates closed at 9am and I had a train to catch for my morning editorial. As you might well empathise, in that moment the thought flashed across my mind that my son was being irrational, spoilt even. Then came the ultimate parental low blow: 'Okay, I'll have to call the headteacher to tell her you are refusing to come to school.' My daughter Clemency, hovering beside me holding her school bag, also began to cry as she realised she would now be late for school.

Brilliant.

Now I had two children in tears, my own stress levels were through the roof, and the thought of what the neighbours were thinking (or how they were judging me) was not exactly helping. On top of all of that, I was cross about having spent good money on school shirts that my son was now refusing to wear.

And then it hit me.

Something was wrong with this equation. I was bearing down on my son – myself an angry baboon – threatening him, trying to force him to do something even though he was clearly in distress. All my training and studies as a children's counsellor had gone out the window, consumed as I was by my own stress and what I saw as my son's unreasonable behaviour.

I took a moment to start over. Never mind being late.

I sat down beside my son and put my arm around him. Wise owl to her owlet. 'Wilbur, what is it about the shirt that you don't like?'

My four-year-old looked at me and through his tears he sobbed.

'We had PE yesterday and I tried to take it off but it was too tight. It got stuck on my head and I couldn't breathe.'

My poor little boy.

My own stress meant my baboon was up and out full throttle before I could consider whether there might be something else going on. In taking a step back and engaging my wise owl, I was able to find my compassion for him in that moment, remembering he is just a small boy who has only been on the planet for a few years. I was able to consider that his behaviour was out of sorts and wonder what was going on. When our children are afraid, their lizard is more likely to kick in, and we'll see that fight–flight or even the freeze response, making it harder still for a young child to articulate themselves clearly. But Wilbur's behaviour should have told me there was something very amiss.

There will **ALWAYS** be a reason underlying your child's behaviour.

And you can _always_ help.

With this book, you are going to become the parental equivalent of Sherlock Holmes, as you use what you learn about your children's brains and how they work, and you can help your children to explain to you how they feel, rather than 'acting it out' instead. Which means, as I said earlier, instead of pondering:

What's wrong with my child?

We can intuitively wonder:

What's going on for them right now? And, most crucially, *how* can I HELP?

No wonder Wilbur did not want to wear the white shirt. With the potential threat to his survival (not being able to breathe), his lizard would have gone into overdrive with it stuck on his head, and that experience would have been lodged as a big NO-NO in his baboon's memory sack. In battling with Wilbur in that moment, I was in danger of fracturing our relationship and the trust he had in me. He doesn't have a wise owl that understands the need to catch a train or get to an editorial meeting; he wouldn't have understood why I was so insistent on him wearing something that he now hated. Our young owlets won't always have the vocabulary or means to articulate what is making them feel the way they do, especially with the lizard in charge, and if they go into panic mode – which is what happened with the shirt – there is no wise owl to explain it to me in slow time. When we understand what's underlying our children's behaviour, we can work *with* them, not *against*.

When we 'wise owl' our children, we help them to self-regulate. With the warmth of our touch and our hugs, with our understanding, we can create for our children the sense that we can not only physically 'hold' them, but that we can hold their big emotions, too. When we model our own calm behaviour, showing our children we can be trusted to help and that we will not shy away from their 'big feelings', their lizard and baboon brains will register this as a 'rewarding' experience and they will come back to us even more readily next time they need our help.

In light of what you now know about your child's developing brain – the lizard, the baboon and the wise owl – let's consider again what the children of those exasperated parents at the start of the chapter might explain to us if they could:

'She's going through the terrible twos!'
Baboon: 'I'm at a crucial stage of my development when I am trying to become more independent but you won't let me!'

'My baby's so clingy.'
Lizard and baboon: 'We're just scared!'

'My daughter can't share.'
'I am a young baboon – if someone takes my food I might not survive – so no, I don't find it easy to share right now.'

'My son's a biter.'
'I'm a lizard who's frightened with a baboon in charge of my body . . . how else can I show how I am feeling? Please tell me how!'

'My twins won't sit still!'
'We are baboons, we need to build up our strength and use our muscles and expend our energy. We NEED to play!'

'Why can't we leave the house on time?!'
Lizard and baboon (looking at each other): 'What's time?'

'My daughter's so ANGRY she keeps hitting her sister.'
'I am a baboon, I act first, think later, I need HELP with my big feelings like rivalry and fear!'

'WHY won't they just DO AS THEY ARE TOLD?!'
'We're baboons . . . we're not fluent in wise Owl.'

And what about those terribly 'well-meaning' people who are always offering unsolicited advice to parents of young children?

'If you keep picking him up, he'll be spoilt/you need to teach baby boundaries to stop him crying.'
I'm a baby with a lizard and baboon driving my behaviour – I'm all about survival, not manipulation!

When we can tap into our own wise owl as parents, it gives us the ability to reflect and help us to make decisions about how WE act and respond to our children in these moments.

Wise Owl Wisdoms

ᵥ ᵛ Your child thinks differently from you because they have a brain that is less developed than yours.

ᵥ ᵛ Symbolically, we will think of our brains as a baobab tree, sending messages and information between our bodies and brains up and down the trunk.

ᵥ ᵛ Sitting in that tree are a (metaphorical) lizard, baboon and wise owl. These different animals are responsible for different aspects of our behaviour.

ᵥ ᵛ As parents, we can help our children's brains develop healthily.

ᵥ ᵛ We can do all that when we see the world as they experience it, <u>through their eyes</u>.

ᵥ ᵛ We can do all that when we use our own wise owl to parent and to regulate our own emotions as much as we help our children to regulate theirs.

Next up – and just as important as what is going on in your child's brain – I will explain what is going on in their body. Our children, without the regulating presence of the wise owl, will often have a FULL BODY REACTION to events that can overwhelm them both physically and mentally. From now on, however, in conjunction with your knowledge of their lizard, baboon and wise owl, you will be able to literally transform their lives – and, dare I whisper it, transform your life, too!

CHAPTER 2

What Goes On in the Brain Doesn't Stay in the Brain

'Stress lives in the body.'

DR NADINE BURKE HARRIS,
paediatrician and Surgeon
General of California

I'm home alone and it's late. The hairs on the back of my neck stand up and I freeze as I hear a tap-tap on the window and realise there is something – or someone – outside. My mind races, the adrenaline surges and my hands clench into fists.

It is in these moments that we experience what is called a stress response and it involves both our lizard and our baboon.

In this situation, I imagine my own lizard sitting vulnerable and exposed at the bottom of the baobab, freezing with fright, making me jump. Meanwhile, my baboon has leapt into action. He's been on high alert anyway, given it is dark and I've been alone, and I imagine him now running along his branch to sound the alarm. He hits what I think of as a big red fire alarm set into the bark of the tree. In reality, in our brains, this is what we know as the amygdala (am-ig-dulla).

> ### Brain Box
>
> 'One of the most important alarm systems is called the amygdala. One of its main functions is to work out the emotional meaning of everything that happens to you. If the amygdala senses that something threatening is happening, it communicates with another structure in the brain called the hypothalamus and this part of the brain actions the release of stress hormones which can then prepare your body for fight–flight.'
>
> Psychotherapist Dr Margot Sunderland, *The Science of Parenting*

When we have these everyday 'stresses', it is processed not just in our heads but in our bodies, too. This is why we experience that fight–flight feeling we might all recognise. The stress hormones adrenaline and cortisol are pumped around our body, priming us to act, firing us up to get ready to do whatever is required. We might get 'butterflies' in our stomach, a dry throat, head fog and, as I had the misfortune to discover in my *Strictly Come Dancing* days, panic-induced foot sweat is also a 'thing'.

It's all part of our stress response or, as scientists call it, our 'limbic hypothalamic adrenal-cortical response'.

We'll just stick with 'STRESS RESPONSE'!

It's a positive thing, designed to keep us alive.

It's what enables us to leap out of the way of a runaway car or flee a burning building. Our stress response helps us hit a deadline, get through a job interview or give a public speech. It helps us cook a meal for ten, run a marathon or head out on a first date.

Stress is healthy in short bursts – in these moments we are designed to be able to focus on overcoming whatever the challenge is, and our body and brain <u>act together as one</u>.

> **Brain Box**
>
> 'We have come to think of "stress" as a bad thing. But it isn't. Stress lets you get things done. It lets you get to work. It lets you navigate the traffic. It lets you learn a new hobby. It lets you fall in love. Stress is when our physiological system is stimulated, whether for positive or negative reasons. When stress comes in bursts, that's healthy. When it lasts for longer, even that is healthy – if you aren't having to handle it entirely alone and you know you have help available.'
>
> Dr Suzanne Zeedyk, infant psychologist, author of *Sabre Tooth Tigers and Teddy Bears: The connected baby guide to attachment*

After this survival response – this big whole-body reaction – our wise owl will then (ideally) step in to soothe and calm the lizard and baboon and switch off the clanging 'fire alarm'. With her beak she hits a green button next to it, what I think of as our body's 'sprinkler' system. In reality, it sends out a flood of anti-anxiety chemicals, 'putting out the fire', as it were.

Our wise owl, our thinking brain, also helps us to work out how best to bring our bodies back to balance practically. We might make ourselves a cup of hot sweet tea after a shock, go for a run after a tough day at the office, pick up the phone to a friend if we've had some bad news or come home and hug our partner after a near-miss crash, seeking comfort in their company and processing what we have been through.

If you are now thinking that YOU might well light a cigarette, have a drink, eat some cake or do some online shopping instead, I hear you! Without being shown ourselves how to deal with stress when WE were younger, we might grow up having found less healthy ways to cope ourselves, which is why we are going to look at how to boost our wise-owl powers in Chapter 14, because it will REALLY help our parenting!

When WE can 'self-regulate', we help our children to regulate as well.

We want to help our children to develop healthy ways of dealing with 'stress', because it is this that underlies so much of that so-called 'naughty' behaviour.

I'll share some very practical and healthy 'coping mechanisms' that will allow you and your children to come back to balance whenever you face a challenge or stress, to recognise what it is you are feeling and manage those 'big emotions' inside. This is what we call having 'emotional regulation' and we'll look at it in detail in Chapter 4.

Let's see how it plays out in my 'Home Alone' scenario.

Whilst my lizard and baboon are doing backflips over this potential threat to my survival, high up in the baobab tree my wise owl has seen that the 'figure' in the garden is actually (hallelujah!) just a fox. It has knocked over the dustbin and is now out there rummaging for food. Thank goodness! My wise owl swoops down from her branch and scoops my leaping lizard and baboon up in the warmth of her feathered wings, reassuring them all is okay. She thanks my two security guards for being so vigilant but explains they can relax and stand down now. Her soothing words and her activation of the sprinkler system helps to restore calm in my mind AS WELL as my body. Thank goodness for my wise owl – I can now make a cup of tea and go to bed with a book, rather than running out of the house in my nightie screaming blue murder.

But what do our children have when they are scared and alone?

They have a fluffy owlet.

And they have *you*.

The world can seem a big old scary place if you have been on the planet for only a short while.

For our babies, whether it's hearing the blender switched on for the first time, being barked at by the puppy or even (and especially) if they are hungry or cold, these will all register as stress or even a potential 'threat' to survival, because to the lizard and baboon they very well might be!

For our young children facing everyday stresses like falling and scraping a knee, having a blood test or being left with a new childcarer, all these things can see a 'whole-body and brain' stress response being triggered.

Without a fully grown wise owl of their own, our children – and especially our babies – need US to bring them back to balance.

When you are there to respond to their cries, with the warmth of your touch, your soothing words and the security they immediately feel when you hold them, their bodies and brains can come back to balance relatively quickly.

But if the stress becomes intolerable, if they are left with that response being activated over and over again, without us to help, it can become harmful. (See Resources for a good source of further information on this topic.)

The stress hormones might then just *sit* in the body (I imagine it like stagnant water) and become what we call 'chronic' or toxic stress, which, as we will soon discover, ain't great. Not for us and definitely not for our children.

'Stress becomes toxic when it is prolonged and when you have no one to help you with it. The adaptations your body has to make to cope with that are not healthy. For children, toxic stress is especially problematic because the ➡

physiological changes it produces can change development. In other words, the toxic stress you experienced as a child can still be affecting your health as an adult. That's why relationships are so very important. Even if a child is coping with seriously challenging things, what matters most is not the stressor but whether you have SOMEBODY to help you with it.'

Dr Suzanne Zeedyk, infant psychologist

It's important to be aware of the impact of chronic/toxic stress, because we know now that when our children's developing brains sit with persistent and unresolved fear it can have lifelong consequences. We know that while we might not cognitively remember every experience from childhood, the stress we might experience during these early years can 'live' in the body and lead to a disruption of the developing architecture of the brain as a result.

Understanding stress and especially how it affects our children's behaviour will help you ENORMOUSLY moving forward. It will empower you to parent more easily and intuitively, using your instincts and this insight. It means you will immediately be able to interpret your children's behaviour, just as I described in Chapter 1.

The main goal of this chapter, before we move on, is to illustrate that *what goes on in our children's brains doesn't just stay in their brains . . . it becomes embedded in their bodies, too.*

Knowing about the stress response and how intensely emotions can be FELT in the body (and brain) will help us moving forward in the book because it sets our children's very physical behaviour into context – the 'naughty' behaviour we might see, such as:

Foot stomping
Screaming
Wailing
Thrashing around
Rolling on the floor
Running away
Fighting

Hmm . . . fight–flight anyone? What else MIGHT we expect from a child without a wise owl to help? What else to do with stress hormones raging – and no other form of release?

Are our children being 'naughty', or are these all natural attempts to release that stress they feel . . . in the only way they know how?

When we understand the stress response, we can see why I say, 'There's No Such Thing as "Naughty".'

When our children are overwrought, when their lizard and baboons are doing backflips with fear, when they don't have a full-grown wise owl to set off those naturally calming chemicals in the body . . . well, what ELSE might we expect them to do?!

As Dr Nadine Burke Harris said at the start of this chapter, 'Stress LIVES in the body.'

Unless we help our children let it out.

Our children's fluffy owlet will become strong and more capable when we are there to show it how. That's when we achieve our all-important goal of helping our children to have 'EMOTIONAL REGULATION'. And our children are going to NEED that because life is not always in balance. Life is more likely to be a series of ups and downs, and we are all sadly likely to experience difficulties, whether in the form of hardship, tragedy or adversity.

We cannot always spare our children the pain of such experiences, much as we might like to.

But when we act as a 'buffer', as a safe place for them to be able to release their big emotions and stress, there is much scientific research to reassure us that they can then overcome many of life's difficult challenges – even the very toughest . . . IF they have us to help them through.

We can move forward into the book proper now, looking at all the scenarios where once we might have assumed our children were being 'naughty', but where we now might recognise they simply need our *help*.

Because as we have seen in this chapter, stress is a whole-body experience, and without a wise owl to 'turn the dial down' the feelings that arise in our children as a result of that stress response can feel REALLY, REALLY BIG and they might explode, without limitation. As Dr Margot Sunderland puts it in her excellent book, *The Science of Parenting*: 'When the alarm systems in the brain are triggered in a child's lower brain, they will be in a state of emotional pain and intense bodily arousal, unless an adult helps them to calm down. This is because once one of the alarm systems has triggered, neurochemical and hormone forces will be activated which overwhelm their mind and body like wildfire.'

And that, ladies and gentlemen, leads to what old-school parenting labels a 'tantrum', which is precisely what we are about to tackle!

Wise Owl Wisdoms

- When we feel under threat, our body is designed to respond.
- That response is both a brain and whole-body reaction.
- Understanding the whole-body reaction enables us to help our children, rather than simply labelling them as 'naughty'.
- Our natural stress response is positive; it is designed to keep us alive. But if the stress response is triggered over longer and sustained periods, it can be damaging to our health – and especially to our children's health, possibly even for the long term.
- With our help and support, our children's stress response can be brought 'back to balance'.
- With our help, our children can learn how to regulate their 'big feelings', and that in turn helps us as parents, too.

All of this is going to lead to you having a much more magical parenting experience, because the more we do this the fewer meltdowns and 'naughty' behaviour we will see, setting up healthy connections in the brain and building an incredible bond of trust and love between you and your child.

PART II

Parenting – the Lizard, the Baboon and the Wise Owl Way

So, now you know about the lizard, the baboon and the wise owl, as well as the whole-body reaction of your child to stress, we can move on to Part II, where we'll look at HOW your children communicate what it is they feel inside, how their emotions drive their behaviour, and how these emotions are expressed. We will look at how to help them to communicate what it is they are feeling and, in summary, conclude that where old-school parenting would once have labelled our children as 'naughty', we now know that was wrong.

There's no such thing as 'naughty' – our children just have needs.

Let's begin, and where better to start than that universal parenting trial: tantrums.

CHAPTER 3

How to Tackle Tantrums and Stop SN-O-T at 20 Paces

*'When little people are overwhelmed
by big emotions, it is our job to share
our calm, not join their chaos.'*

L.R. KNOST, author and children's advocate

When Wilbur went wild at the wild nursery

When my son was three and a half, he attended a 'wild nursery'
in the woods near our home. Each day he would play to his heart's
content in a big red onesie ski suit, which protected him from the
mud and damp. His teachers would make fires and dens and show
the kids the wonders of Nature and all that she brings.

At pick-up time, I would stand at a gate that opened on to the
forest alongside the other parents, all peering over to see which

'onesie' was ours. When Wilbur saw me, he would run at full pelt, his red ski suit so covered in mud that I could barely tell the colour of it, holding a stick or maybe a jam jar filled with leaves, earwigs or other such delicious delights. In return, I would always bring something for him – an apple, a clementine, perhaps a banana – a small fruit-sugar boost before lunchtime, but also a little ritual offering between mother and son.

On this particular day, Wilbur ran towards me as usual but the look on his face was strained. I sensed something was up but, as always, I stood grinning with joy, arms outstretched, apple in hand, to welcome my boy back to me. However, instead of mirroring me as he would usually do, his face contorted into a raging snarl.

'You said you would bring me an orange! I WANT an orange!'

With that, Wilbur threw himself to the ground, fists flailing in the mud. Wow! . . . Cue red flush under my cheeks. In front of all the other parents . . . my son had rejected me! My lizard and baboon went wild.

My first instinct was to **FIGHT**. I wanted to meet my son's rage head-on and tell him off for sounding so spoilt. I could have dragged my three-year-old kicking, squirming and screaming to the car, fighting to get him into the car seat, flaring up a battle of wills with both of us upset all the way home. But an enraged me, shouting at my son in public, did not feel so great.

My lizard and baboon thought I should perhaps **FLEE!** I wanted to get out of there fast without actually trying to get to the bottom of his upset, which would have just changed the location without finding a solution. Besides, given that Wilbur was prostrate on the muddy ground and didn't look like getting up any time soon, that wasn't such a good look either!

There *had* to be another way? My lizard threw up one last option: Ta-daa! **FREEZE!**

Maybe I could just ignore him and hope the tantrum would 'go away'?

Except this didn't look like it *would* just 'go away'. Doing nothing would have . . . done nothing.

I felt all eyes on me as the other children raced through the gate, happy and smiling into their parent's arms. I suspected half the adults were thinking: *Wow! So spoilt!*, while the other half winced, *Thank God it's not me.*

This scenario *may* feel a little familiar! To paraphrase a well-known saying: 65 per cent of parents admit to their young child having had at least one tantrum, the other 35 per cent aren't telling the truth! All of us <u>will</u> be faced with this dilemma at some point in these early years and, especially when it is a public meltdown, not only is it likely to provoke the 'fight–flight, freeze or faint' response in us, but it usually also triggers our self-doubt too:

'Why is everyone else's kid happy to see them?'

'Am I a terrible parent?'

Or worse still . . .

'Is there something wrong with my child?'

By now I hope you will already anticipate my answer: NO!

Remember: for a child under five, **there is no such thing as 'naughty'!**

There is nothing wrong with your child – and nothing wrong with you.

Brain Box

'Tantrums happen when a child is feeling overwhelmed by an intense emotion that they aren't able to process. Whilst a tantrum can be sparked by many different reasons, the underlying issue is that a child is expressing an emotion which is "too big", unknown, unmanageable, and overwhelming. It could be frustration, a desire to be more independent, a scary new experience, jealousy, or anger, etc. Letting it all out by having a tantrum is the way they feel able to express how they feel. Some children might also have a tantrum as a way to be "seen", and to get the attention they crave. It's important to remember that, no matter how trivial the reason for the tantrum may seem to you, it is a real and important feeling to them. As they get older, we can show our children how to express their feelings in a safe way. It's a gradual process. They will learn these things as time goes by, but the only way to really work this out is for them to start having the tantrums to begin with.'

Dr Camilla Rosan, head of Early Years Service at the Anna Freud National Centre for Children and Families

In reality, tantrums simply tell us that our children are *overwhelmed*: they might feel overwhelmed because they are tired; maybe because they were having fun at the playground and can't easily switch to 'going home now'; they might feel overwhelmed because earlier in the day their sister took their favourite toy and broke it and you weren't there to tell her off; or perhaps they are overwhelmed because they're bored and their brain is in a state of arousal that they haven't yet developed the ability to cope with.

As we saw in Chapter 2, when our children under five feel threatened, frightened or 'wronged' – even if the actual incident is in reality quite minor – their ancient brain will take over and that STRESS RESPONSE gets triggered. As you now know, their wise owl isn't sufficiently well developed yet to rationalise the situation for them, so the lizard and baboon are in control.

* * *

Back in the wild nursery, a little baboon in his red, mud-splattered ski suit was still writhing around in the dirt. I took a step back and grappled with my thoughts. It bought me enough time for my own wise owl to cut through.

Hold on. Wilbur's always so happy to see me. He was fine this morning, now he's not. What if this isn't about the apple?

Then the lightning-bolt moment . . .

This is not about me. Something must have happened . . .

The minute I was able to take a step back, pause for thought and let my wise owl brain take charge, I was able to see things from Wilbur's perspective, not just my own. Instead of feeling frustration, embarrassment, even anger at my little boy's behaviour, I was instead flooded with compassion for him.

The science of 'temper tantrums'

As we saw in Chapter 1, our young children are, in effect, 'blank books' when it comes to experience. Every day's a school day, as it were. They can only process new experiences in the 'here and now' using their baboon, that ancient mammalian brain designed to respond quickly when it feels under threat or 'wronged'. This is exacerbated if Mum or Dad aren't there, which is increasingly the case for longer periods in the modern world (I will come back to this topic in Chapter 10). This means our children face a lot of life's new experiences without us being there, without us by their side to help.

As we saw in the previous chapter, we adults might not interpret incidents as threatening because we have decades of experience to give us perspective. For a child at this stage of brain development, another child coming at them with a raised fist, even during 'play', can feel like a threat, and their bodies will react accordingly and that stress response will kick in.

The thing is, fight–flight, freeze or faint are not always options for our little ones, so what else can they do? Our young children might not be confident enough yet to find a teacher to help them, or even be able to articulate how they feel. Thus they might be forced to swallow and suppress all those new feelings. And, guess what? As we saw in Chapter 2, stress is not merely a *feeling*. Stress **lives** in the body in the form of stress hormones that flood the body via the bloodstream. Can you imagine now how that might feel for your child under five?

Think about times when you've felt stressed, perhaps before

getting up to give a speech, doing a job interview or doing anything challenging for the first time. Like our kids, our bodies
respond, too: we might lose the desire to eat, we have 'butterflies',
we get brain fog, our breathing is shallower, we might even feel
light-headed. When we have a build-up of stress, how might we let
it out? Might we go for a run, work-out at the gym or do something
active to literally release what we feel inside?

But as I said in the previous chapter, what about your children?
They have no way of letting that stress out, perhaps not until they
feel safe enough to do so . . .

And guess when that might be?

And who might that be with?

Yes! When <u>you</u> come to collect them.

When they see <u>you</u>, their *safe haven*, the person they trust the
most in all the world.

Except, when we see our children's behaviour as a 'tantrum' as
something 'naughty', what do we do?

We PUNISH them.

Just when they need us the most.

* * *

Back at the wild nursery, a three-year-old Wilbur is still knee
(and face) deep in the mud. What do you see now? A 'naughty',
spoilt little boy kicking off about an orange? Or a child in need

of comfort? A child who has been overwhelmed by something, both physically and psychologically? A child whose 'fire alarm' has gone off big-style and, trust me, it ain't about an orange.

I admit that I was *still* mortified that this was all taking place in front of everyone, but with my wise owl brain now in charge, I suddenly felt confident that I knew what to do.

I knelt down to Wilbur's level on the mud beside him, and in a slightly louder voice than usual, I exclaimed:

'Ohhh!' (as though I'd just twigged something – silly me!)

The sing-song tone of my voice was enough to cut through.

Wilbur looked up.

'Oh! Silly Mummy! You wanted an orange?!' I said, as if the thought had just occurred to me.

In a situation like this, you need to use as few words as possible: Wilbur's baboon was still very much in charge of his behaviour, so I had to cut through and connect. With the word 'orange', I saw it register.

Ah! She understands me!

His baboon was stopped in its tracks. By using the one word Wilbur had said was most important to him at that very moment, I had connected with him. Regardless of what was really going on, in that moment we had connected and I knew I had to act quickly.

Reaching out my hand, I asked if he wanted to come with me. I was amazed when his tears stopped and he just stood up! I felt like taking a little bow, so incredible was the transformation! My own lizard was doing backflips, but with my little man's hand in mine, I relaxed as we moved away from the crowd. Now that I had Wilbur's full attention, for added effect I took the apple and bonked myself on the head with it.

'Silly Mummy, look, Wilbur, the apple is telling me, "Silly Mummy!"'

Wilbur giggled.

Another bonk on the head; this time switching to a silly squeaky 'apple' voice, I pretended it was cross with me.

'Wilbur wanted an orange! WHY did you bring ME!?'

Wilbur's roar of laughter was like medicine. The humour released our tension and lifted us both. We ran back along the path together, laughing as I built upon the apple animation, holding it out in front of me, telling me how silly I was today and didn't I know that we had oranges at home. 'The apple' then asked Wilbur if he wanted to go play in the leaves and he gleefully grabbed it from my hand, taking a bite as he pulled me towards the big pile of leaves saying, 'Come, Mummy, play!'

His relief to me seemed palpable. Something had shifted in our relationship: a sense of a deepening bond between mother and son. It felt like something profound had happened. My three-year-old had realised that *Mummy could hold his pain* even when it felt like the worst feeling in the world and, better still, she would not get cross with him.

I was so exhilarated and in love with him at that moment that I had no problem rolling around in those leaves right down in the mud with him. Looking back now, I could see that it was a great stress reliever for me, too, thrashing around in leaves and laughing – what better way to give both our stressed-out bodies an outlet?

So, let's now take a moment to consider this 'temper tantrum' again.

We had a massive meltdown by a three-year-old. Sounds familiar? When that happens – especially when it happens in public – our own primitive baboon is likely to be triggered. That's because we ourselves feel under threat – in this case, the threat is in feeling shamed in public by our own child. The shame and guilt of looking like a bad or incompetent parent.

The problem is that when our lizard and baboon are triggered, our own stress response kicks in and we typically resort to fight–flight, freeze or faint ourselves.

HOWEVER, if you can override your lizard and baboon and engage the wise owl, your ability to handle your child's tantrums in an empathetic and caring way will be TRANSFORMED. In that moment of hideousness, take a breath and allow your wise owl to take charge, and very quickly your lizard and baboon will quietly stand down. Then you'll be able to survey the scene calmly from a different perspective: *the perspective of your child in that moment.*

Stay with me for a moment. Let's say something happened at your workplace that upset you: perhaps your boss had dressed you down or a colleague had spoken behind your back or criticised your work. More than likely you might have bottled up your feelings, and then when you got home and needed to offload you would've told your parent, friend or partner.

However, imagine if instead of listening to you and offering support, they had either shrugged it off, simply ignored you or, perhaps worst of all, told you not to be so ridiculous or silly.

How would you feel? How might that affect your relationship moving forward?

By really HEARING and SEEING our children in their moment of distress, we are meeting them with compassion and understanding, which helps us to not only bring our children back from the brink of a meltdown, but it also helps us to form an even stronger bond with them.

There is an added bonus – dealing with tantrums in this way also helps your child's brain development. Each time we soothe and comfort our children in their distress, we are helping to build and develop the all-important skills of emotional self-regulation that I will talk about in Chapter 4.

All of this we can do when we accept THERE IS NO SUCH THING AS 'NAUGHTY'.

On that particular day at the wild nursery, I still wanted to get to the bottom of what had *caused* Wilbur's reaction. After releasing the stress with our play in the leaves, we walked to the car. Only then did I feel able to ask him,

'Sunshine, it seems like you had some pretty big feelings there – how was everything today?'

Wilbur paused. He stopped and looked at me. 'Max pushed me.'

'Oh, Wilbur, what happened, sweetheart?'

'He pushed me in the mud.'

Ahhh … and that was it right there. The threat that triggered Wilbur's stress response and fired up a whole-body response.

But there was more. Looking at me directly, he said accusingly, 'Where were you?'

And POW! Just like that, I understood.

He had faced a difficult experience at nursery and he'd had to cope with it alone. In that moment, I understood that he had held in all that stress as a result of what had happened, all the rough and tumble of play, the decisions he'd had to make about how to respond … nursing his hurt and holding it all in until he saw me – his safe haven, his safe wise owl – someone who could scoop him up and make everything better.

I had been slightly late that day for pick-up and I imagined him looking out for me, watching all the other parents arrive, but not <u>his</u> mum. All his emotions, stored up inside, ready to let loose … but I wasn't there! His emotions had boiled over like the pot on the nursery fire. I needed to own that, not him: *my brain* is fully formed and functioning. I can reason all of this out in just a few seconds. Wilbur is only just starting out in this life where bad stuff sometimes happens and we miss those who can keep us safe.

'Oh, sweetheart, that sounds tough. That is not acceptable behaviour and I am so sorry I was not there for you.' We stopped in our tracks and I knelt down again to look at him directly.

'Mummy is so sorry she wasn't there. That must have been really tough.'

I can't know in that moment exactly what had happened that day at nursery. It might likely just have been over-exuberant play because Max is, just like Wilbur, an over-excited baboon himself. It does not really matter, what is more important in that moment was how I <u>responded</u> as a parent. Life is not without challenge, and social interactions can provide important learning opportunities for our young children. But when they are starting out, they might need our help to show them what to do if we are not around.

'Okay, darling, Mummy understands. The next time there is too much rough play, do you think you can find your teacher to tell them?'

Wilbur looked a little sceptical. 'Or do you think you can use the word, "STOP!" and say, "I don't like this game, now"?'

Wilbur nodded. He still seemed a little unsure, and I didn't want to push it, although I made a mental note to mention it to his teacher so that she could help him navigate it if it did happen again.

We cannot expect our very young children to have to manage difficult social interactions alone. We must model the solutions for them so they can learn about conflict resolution and how to feel able to lay boundaries around behaviour, to feel able to state to other children what is, and is not, acceptable. To know they can tell other children to STOP and, if they really need to, know that they can take the issue to a teacher for help.

I knew Wilbur might not necessarily process all of this in that moment, as there was a lot to take in. But by hearing my son, seeing his distress and acknowledging it, I was doing something equally important. I was letting him know that it is okay to feel upset when things upset us; it is okay to feel anger – that is a valid emotion which is triggered when we feel we've been wronged. And by me owning it, rather than asking Wilbur to take the blame for the meltdown, I was letting him know he could come to me next time and tell me something was wrong, rather than resorting to another 'tantrum' face down in the mud.

Wilbur cried then – another wonderful stress release, as I will talk about in Chapter 5. Finally, we hugged, with a surge of oxytocin, the 'love drug' that is released when there is physical contact between a parent and their child – or between any two people who love each other, come to that. Then we stood up and walked, hand in hand, to head home.

And do you know what? Wilbur ate the apple just fine.

Okay, so let's introduce the first tool in our parenting Tool Kit!

TOOL KIT TIP

Stop SN-O-T!

When faced by a tantrum in public or at home:

- We must first **STOP!**

- *Take a breath and pause.*

Remind yourself *this is not personal*; this is not your child being a dark arts master! And they are NOT being 'naughty', manipulative, stubborn, testing ... etc., whatever the old school of parenting might try to tell you. They are not capable of that.

- Then remember **that it's:**

  S'Not about you – this is NOT personal: your child might be in the middle of a stress response triggered by something else entirely.

  O – OBSERVE: so what else could be going on?

  T – TURN IT AROUND: think about the situation from the perspective of your child.

  (Doing this will also engage your wise-owl brain, rather than see you steaming into battle with your own baboon.)

Practical examples for using STOP SN-O-T: when our under-fives won't do as we ask!

1 The oily pushchair octopus

What to do when your child refuses to get in or out of the pushchair – triggering a tantrum?

Well, for starters, let's **STOP!**

For our very young children – which they will be if they are in a pram – we must remember this is **SN'ot** personal.

Your little one is not thinking: *I know, I will refuse to get in the pushchair, I will really resist, because that will wind 'em up.*

Of course they aren't!

As you now know, between the age of one and three, your child has a baboon brain in charge, a baboon that is starting to take an interest in the world and needs some independence. The baboon knows: *I have more chance of surviving if I can build up my muscles and walk. I need to understand where the world is and I want to have some control over what I'm doing, so* **PLEASE** *let me!*

So how best to address?

OPTION ONE

Well, once we have taken a moment to **STOP** and get our wise-owl thinking cap on, we can make an assessment and perhaps think: *Hmm, is it really such a big deal if she walks?*

OBSERVE We're in a safe environment; that is, not near a busy main road, so let your child know you understand them, which is the first step to the baboon calming down: she has been *heard*.

'Oh, Maisie, I can SEE how much fun it is to walk! You want to walk?!'

The use of the word 'walk' here has the same potency as the word 'orange' did with Wilbur – you are demonstrating to your child that you 'get it'.

For extra effect, you might even add with a smile, 'Gosh, I can see you *really, really* want to walk!'

You can smile when you know the situation is not personal – when you don't take this as a slight or challenge to your leadership. When we can use our wise owl thinking, we realise this might be about our child's baboon brain needing to burn off some energy or gain some independence; it helps us think with a different perspective and get a win–win.

Now you can **TURN IT AROUND.**

Speak as though you are indeed talking to that baboon – calm and with very few words so it doesn't get excited again. You might want to crouch down to her level so you are not looming over her, triggering that baboon 'stress' response. Keep smiling . . .

'Daddy/Mummy UNDERSTANDS! I know how GOOD you are at walking!'

NOW you'll really have her attention. Her baboon might have been anticipating a battle in this moment, but now she can relax, leaving you more able to engage with your child's growing fluffy owlet instead. In this moment, when things are more calm, you can decide double quick: is this a battle I need to have?

You might think that actually it does no harm for her to walk; in fact, it's rather sweet that she's gaining some confidence and, on reflection, it will make her more tired for bedtime. Maybe you can hold her hand and chat as you go. I guarantee she will be content to do so (just like when Wilbur was suddenly happy to take the apple) as your child senses you really do understand them.

You can then relax and enjoy your time together. Okay, so it might take a bit longer to get home, but hey, this is a chance for some magical bonding with your little baboon, who is going to love you all the more!

OR ...

OPTION TWO

You are thinking: *Well, this is all well and good, and I get it, but we ARE near a really busy road and that's stressing me out, plus we REALLY DO NEED TO GET HOME!*

Well, let's still **STOP SN-O-T**!

This time we might have to bring in a boundary to help us: a gentle limit that lets your baboon know, 'Okay, I hear you and I see you, but I have to draw a line on this because it's not that safe right now.' Laying boundaries does *not* mean forcing your child into the pushchair, because that does nothing but pit two angry baboons against each other – you will obviously succeed, but you won't 'win'.

Forcing/fighting will do nothing to bond your little family unit.

But using gentle boundaries and humour will.

So let's go back to **STOP SN-O-T**!

We **STOP** and engage our wise owl brain.

We know it is **S'not** about us, so we don't have to take this as a personal challenge.

OBSERVE

I wish I could say yes, but it feels too dangerous.

In which case you can say:

'Okay! But the road is too noisy (you could put your hands over your ears and make a crazy sound to make her laugh) and there are too many cars . . . (another silly motion) BUT we CAN definitely walk when we get to our street . . . deal?!'

If she's still upset, just repeat . . . using fewer words, just so she hears through the white noise of the tantrum, 'Yes, you CAN walk! Just when we get away from the big smelly cars!'

Her baboon hears the word CAN. It's not about a fight on the baboon's part, remember, so the boundary is not going to freak her out, all she needs to know is that you understand her need to walk and she can do it soon!

Now you've **TURNED IT AROUND.**

Using humour helps to defuse that full-body stress response, and using boundaries helps your child to feel safe. We will talk about boundaries in more detail in Chapter 8. In this example, it simply means calmly drawing a line around what is and is not possible, but you are explaining it because you need to keep her SAFE. This is something that can resonate with the baboon because she's all about survival, remember? And however young your child is, they know what it means to feel safe.

In this exchange, you can not only calm the baboon but you can also encourage your daughter's own little owl to grow in stature, as she has to think about and ponder the solution you have now offered. All good for brain development and certainly all good for the future when we'll need to solve problems bigger than strapping our kids into prams! By giving your child a choice as well as something to consider, it engages the 'seeking' part of their brain, part of her fluffy owlet, helping it to grow. All being well, you will then get a little girl who climbs into the pram happily, until you get to the end of the street when she knows she can walk as part of the 'deal'.

This is about you being inventive, about you working with your child to find a solution.

Don't see these exchanges as you giving in. This is not about being a 'weak' parent.

Quite the opposite. It's been shown that in many areas of life – in business, in leadership, from big corporations down to the family unit – time and again, empathy and collaboration get the best results. When interviewing entrepreneur and author Margaret Heffernan, she spoke to me about the enormous amount of research to support that collaboration is the BEST form of leadership and produces the best results whether we are talking about business or family life.

Let's take another example before we move on.

2 My child won't leave the park when we need to go home

Okay, hopefully, you now know what to do:

STOP

Take a moment.

It's **S'Not** personal. Your child is not thinking: *I am going to make*

Daddy's life really difficult. I know he has to get back for a work call/ to cook supper, so I will be 'naughty' here and refuse to come back when he calls.

Of course he isn't!

With a baboon in charge of his brain, what is your child actually thinking?

I'm having FUN! I live in the present. I don't understand time or work calls or how long it takes to prepare my tea. I'm on overdrive right now! Why would I WANT to leave the park while it's so good?

OBSERVE

My little boy was having such a joyful time and now I am ending it mid-flow. By looking at things from his perspective, you can now empathise with him! He's not being 'naughty' – he was just having fun. 'Oh, Ollie, I am so SORRY! I can see you are having SO MUCH **FUN!**'

Again, use a sing-song voice and smile when you speak to him.

'Daddy understands! It's SO much fun here in the park with your friends, isn't it?'

(You can repeat this for good measure so you really have that baboon calmed down and on board – don't worry about how 'over the top' you sound to anyone else, if you are genuine with your empathy, your child will listen.)

'It's hard, but we have to go now.'

And <u>there</u> is the boundary, softly lobbed in. You are letting him know you understand his **DISAPPOINTMENT** and how hard it is to have to leave. But you still have to go.

Let's be realistic here: it still might be hard for him to leave. He is having as much of a STRESS RESPONSE in his body when he is having fun as he is when he is having a tough time. As we will see in Chapter 4, the feeling of joy in the body can be equally over-whelming an experience for little ones. So, don't worry if there are tears. I think of tears as stress leaving the body! You might even want to add a dollop of extra empathy here if your child is REALLY upset about having to stop what they are doing. If, in these moments, your child cries even harder when you are sooth-ing them, remember: it's a sure sign of that stress being released.

Now we can **TURN IT AROUND.**

Here you can lay a boundary, offering your child another five minutes to help give them a buffer period for their baboon to calm down. You can even shake hands on it.

Again, you might kneel down so you are not looming over your child, making that stress response worse. Use a soothing voice. Don't worry about other people looking – it's none of their busi-ness! Trust me, it will work – just keep going. I accept that when you do this for the first time, especially if you are in public, it can seem hard to know what best to say or you might worry about saying 'the wrong thing'. Just keep your sentences short, be sincere and show that you are intent on helping your child with their pain. They will sense your sincerity and they will trust you even if you miss the mark when you first start trying to decipher what might be going on.

Rather than this being a difficult experience for you as a parent, it is in fact an OPPORTUNITY. An opportunity to better understand your child and to strengthen the relationship you have with them. I appreciate it can often feel difficult, especially when we ourselves might be feeling stressed, thinking about work emails that need answering, dinner to get ready, about taking some time for ourselves! But if we can STOP in these moments and attune to our children, when we respond calmly and with compassion, our children will feel closer to us and want to collaborate, because the exchange has literally soothed their brains – in fact, science can show us that positive connections will be made in the brain as a result. It feels good when we put our arms around our children and say, 'It's okay, I understand.'

It is in these moments that the magic happens.

Because it is in these moments that you are helping your child to experience all-important EMPATHY, that is, our ability to understand and relate to what other people are feeling, thinking and what they might be experiencing emotionally. Empathy is crucial if our children are to become (wise owl) adults who care for other people's well-being, who act with compassion, who get along with others and, on an even wider scale, for a future generation to thrive as a healthy society. Julie Harmieson, co-director of Trauma Informed Schools explains, 'Empathy is not a developmental skill we just acquire. It is hard to teach it, we have to experience it.'

When we respond to our children empathically, using a wise owl approach, we are helping them to *experience* that feeling of being comforted. It 'lights' up the brain and helps our children to become empathic in their own right, because they will recognise how good it feels and want to do the same for others in turn. We will have children who naturally want to alleviate pain and suffering in others, and who will relate more sensitively to other people's well-being. In showing our children we can put ourselves in their shoes, to understand how *they* feel in any given moment (especially the more challenging moments!), we are helping that fluffy owlet brain to grow into an emotionally sophisticated 'wise owl' who cannot bear to see another in pain and will always move towards them to help.

Back at the park, Dad is now calm, he has looked at his little boy with the tears streaming down his face and all at once he understands this is genuinely difficult for him. Here's how the conversation might then develop.

'I know, sunshine, it's okay, come here, it's okay, I understand.'

He's almost there then ... 'Come, would you like a cuddle?' Or perhaps he might ask ...

'Would you like me to scoop you up and do an aeroplane?!'

If our children are more used to a big scary baboon response from us in these situations this 'fun dad/mum' response can be enough of a curve ball to see them stop in their tracks! When you offer up another solution, it helps bring that baboon down from his branch, take his hand off that fire alarm as he thinks ... *Hmm that would be fun!*

If aeroplanes are not your thing, you could pose a question to engage that thinking owlet brain. Something like, 'Shall we see how many yellow leaves we can pick up on the way home?'

You might be surprised how quickly your child says YES! The tears will stop as they take your hand, much as Wilbur did with me ... and away you go.

It's such a great feeling when you can defuse a situation in this way! It will work. Just have faith, because I know it can take confidence the first time you try it. But every time you do it, you'll feel the connection between you and your child building what the Harvard Center on the Developing Child describes as that 'serve and return'.

THIS is what builds bonds with our children – the bonds we will have for life.

In that immediate moment, instead of you striding off in anger, feeling like the WORST mum/dad in the world, having wrestled with your child, forcing them into their pram while they are kicking and screaming, you will instead feel you've won first prize in the parenting stakes! Using force does not work. It fractures the relationship we have with our children. It teaches them to suppress their natural urges, push down the healthy behaviour that their brain is urging them to do (e.g. become more independent). Using force teaches your child . . . to use force. Do you really want that when they are older?

As we saw with Wilbur at the wild nursery, when our children have a full-blown stress response (or as old school would label it a 'tantrum'), it can be really rather alarming, scary even. Even if our children are kicking and screaming, as long as they are somewhere that neither you nor they can be injured, you can be confident that by staying with them, not abandoning them in this massive moment of stress, then with your calm presence and your empathy and compassion, that baboon WILL take his hand off the fire alarm, and you can be the wise owl who can bring your child back down to balance. Just let that baboon know you are not going anywhere, that you want to keep them safe and you are there to help . . . and you will most likely see your child crawling into your lap pretty soon after for an all-important restorative hug.

Parent ponders: Claire, mum to two children under five

'It can be exhausting always being "on", always having half-conversations with people when I am out, always being used as a climbing frame. When we are out at the park, I can end up irritated and irate, and whilst all parents feel this desire for their children to behave, being a solo mum, I don't have the old back-up warning of, "Wait till your father gets home." When I reach the end of my tether, I might find myself with one child in meltdown – my son can be quite physical and refuses my hug, which can trigger my own feelings of being rejected. When I feel rejected, so I reject him. What has helped is realising that I am a baboon, too, and just knowing this helps to release my pressure and anxiety, and helps me to become my wise owl quicker and with more humour. When I can make my son laugh, it is as though nothing had previously happened! All is forgiven by us both!'

We can all relate, I imagine, to Claire's dilemma. Not only can it feel quite scary when our children are in distress, and kicking and screaming and refusing our help, but it can also leave us feeling rather helpless, rejected and, dare I say, inadequate, too – there goes that old guilt trip again! So, in these moments remember, just as your child is clearly feeling some BIG emotions inside, so will you. Yours might be suppressed because you have a wise owl that will caution you not to kick and scream in public yourself (!) but you can still have those feelings created by that stress response we looked at in Chapter 2.

Distraction in those moments when everyone is in 'overwhelm' is a super-helpful tool to have up your sleeve – distractions that use humour and are wonderfully silly can often work really well. Children love nonsense and funny observations and anything designed to make your little one laugh: for example, the speaking apple or an 'oh look at that dog sniffing that man's bottom' (apologies to the gentleman concerned), but, honestly, take it to any level of silliness – your children will love you for it and it's such a great release and is often enough, in that split second, to stop the baboon in his tracks and have him rolling around with laughter. He can't be mad at you and laughing at the same time! A lot of this will be trial and error but I guarantee when you find something that works for you and your child it will feel AMAZING!

'When we understand the WHY, we can deal with the WHAT.'

Please know that this will all get so much easier over time; the more you take these opportunities for a moment to bond with your child, so the trust between you will build and build. The more you do it, the fewer tantrums you will see. And the bonus is this scientific fact: over time and with enough repetition, neural connections will be made in their developing brains so the 'tantrums' will get fewer and further between. All the memories of the time 'Dad/Mum helped me to manage my big feelings' get stored in the baboon's memory sack. All to the power of good!

When we force our children to comply, we stand to lose their trust, they WILL grow up to resist us, to rebel against us and do the very things that we don't want them to do. They will just do them behind our backs, when we are not looking. When you work *with* that little baboon, you will not only be laying the foundation for a child that graduates to having a wise owl, too, rich in rational thought, impulse control, empathy and resilience, but you are strengthening the foundation between you and building an unbreakable bond. These experiences form the building blocks of your child's future mental health, emotional well-being, resilience, and the connection they will *always* have with you. You can either fight them all the way and build up a wall of resistance between you both – or work with that developing brain and help it grow in the best way possible. *Our response as parents will be key in helping them to communicate how they feel in the future.*

Wise Owl Wisdoms

ᵥ ᵛ Tantrums are a sure sign that our children's bodies and brains have been overwhelmed.

ᵥ ᵛ They are most often a sign that our children are responding to a threat, perceived or otherwise, and the feelings that arise inside them are genuinely stressful.

ᵥ ᵛ We can switch into wise owl mode ourselves when we see our children not as 'naughty' but rather that they have been 'hijacked' by a full-body stress response.

ᵥ ᵛ In these moments, instead of battling baboon to baboon, we can use them as opportunities to help our children grow their wise owl. To do that we need to deploy our own wise owl, too.

ᵥ ᵛ Remember, when a scenario with your child occurs and it feels like an emergency, BEFORE your baboon gets into gear think: **STOP SN-O-T!**

ᵥ ᵛ **STOP SN-O-T** allows us to pause, remind ourselves it is not about us, then turn things around.

ᵥ ᵛ Wise Owl Parenting means you allow your child to experience EMPATHY, which is VITAL to their individual growth and social well-being.

Our capacity to love is based on our ability to stand in someone else's shoes, to care about their circumstances and want to alleviate their pain and distress. For me, showing our children we genuinely *care* about them in these moments, using our wise owl parenting, is critical – because we are showing our children how to love.

CHAPTER 4

Emotional Regulation
and SAS Parenting

*'We need to foster emotional
competence in our children, as the
best preventative medicine.'*

DR GABOR MATÉ, renowned speaker,
author and addiction expert

A surgeon once told me that while he was a junior doctor a former
colleague took a scalpel to a fellow medic's throat in a fit of rage.
This is a classic example of a baboon (in a grown-up body) going
on the rampage!

When we see an adult with their baboon in
charge, whether we are parents shouting at our
children, or a surgeon with a scalpel in his hand,
it's a sure sign we are not practising our own
emotional regulation.

We probably all know someone in our day-to-day lives who has a reputation for flying 'off the handle' at the slightest bit of pressure. If we're honest, most of us have been there, too, especially when we are tired or stressed ourselves. We might find ourselves in baboon mode when our children won't listen to us or when they're fighting (again) and it's late, and we're tired and at our wits' end.

In baboon mode, we might respond by yelling at our children, even though it's not fair or appropriate. We can all over-react to situations when we are tired or stressed and our baboons take over, not with a scalpel (I hope not!) . . . but you get my drift. So, we shouldn't be surprised if our children do the same, too.

Hopefully, as adults with our wise owls, we can usually manage our big feelings, take a step back and breathe . . . maybe consider that the children are just tired after a long day at school and they simply need to run off some steam. We can reflect that the stress we are feeling might be more likely due to the work email we perhaps received just five minutes before. It's not about the children at all. In these moments I can now find myself calm and can offer to read a book with them, deciding the email can wait until after they are asleep.

This is the art of **EMOTIONAL REGULATION** *and it's one of the single most precious things we can gift our children in these first five years.* But what actually is an EMOTION?

It's a good question.

So, emotions are fleeting but often very intense feelings that are directed at someone or something, in response to what we feel inside or due to something we experience. Here's the *Oxford Dictionary* definition: 'A strong feeling deriving from one's circumstances, mood, or relationships with others.' Emotions have their roots in evolution (as always!), in that they drive our behaviour to help us adapt to our environment in order to keep us alive. Again, it's all about *survival*.

And it is your – and your child's – ability to MANAGE those emotions that will have an enormous impact on their lives (and yours).

If you can manage your emotions, and teach your child how to manage theirs, then rather than 'act out' big feelings (like the surgeon with the scalpel), you can express them in more appropriate and healthy ways.

In order to regulate our emotions, first it is worth us looking at the key emotions that will impact on you and your child's daily lives, so that you are better equipped to respond appropriately when those emotions cause a reaction from them. Psychologists Dr Paul Ekman and Dr Robert Plutchik suggest there are a number of primary emotions, which are also the foundation for many more secondary emotions. Indeed, some sources suggest we can experience 34,000 different emotions. I'm not so sure we need to go through all of them here – you know me by now, I like to keep things simple. It is generally accepted by psychologists and child development specialists that the core emotions include, but are not limited to:

Happiness
Sadness
Fear
Anger
Surprise
Disgust

These are the primary colours, if you like, from which all those other thousands of emotions are an offshoot. You can obviously see your young child ripping open a Christmas present with enormous excitement as a perfect example of an intensely joyous feeling of happiness. Likewise, if their beloved pet hamster goes to the great wheel in the sky, they will experience sadness. A loud bang outside their playroom will create fear and surprise, while a child at nursery smashing over the greatest Lego tower ever built will certainly solicit anger. Disgust is an emotion we might recognise in our children's faces when we hand them a plate of 'Mummy's new supper experiment' or even perhaps when watching someone else's inappropriate behaviour (picking our nose, anyone?).

The secondary emotions that can be experienced by all of us include, but again are not limited to, feelings such as shame, jealousy, disappointment, guilt, rage, loss, and so on. These can actually be very pernicious and in parenting we must be very aware of them. For example, shame is often used in punishments – sitting a child on a 'naughty step' or making them stand in the corner of the classroom – but shame is a very negative emotion to evoke in a child. It might curtail their behaviour, but it gives them a very negative sense of themselves, making them think they are not good enough as they are. If a child who is angry is punished by being shamed, he will likely become an adult who associates anger with shame.

Another example might be if we were chastised by our parents when we were joyful – perhaps told off or punished for running around the house with glee – then we might come to associate joy with fear and, as a result, that can limit our reaction to happy events in the future. And for those of us with siblings, jealousy is felt as a very strong emotion – one borne from fear: the fear of, *Mum/Dad loving my sibling more than me.*

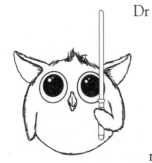

Dr Plutchik developed a visual tool called an Emotion Wheel to help us visualise these emotions a little more clearly, as well as the relationship between these primary and secondary emotions (I reference his work at the back of the book if you would like to delve in a little deeper). Or I might refer you to an alternative 'expert' – in *Star Wars*, Master Yoda explained the emotional chain of events rather well when he said, 'Fear leads to anger, anger leads to hate, hate leads to suffering.'

Before I move on to ways that you can help your child manage their emotions, let me first make one VERY CRUCIAL point about babies and emotions. It might be tempting to think that when we are staring at our phones, next to our gorgeous, gurgling bundle of joy, that they aren't feeling emotions in a way that older children or adults do. But babies can feel emotions, and those feelings can be VERY INTENSE, as infant psychologist Dr Suzanne Zeedyk explains in her book, *Sabre Tooth Tigers and Teddy Bears*, using shame as an example: 'Shame comes out of experiences a child has with other people. If a parent doesn't respond when the child cries or offer support for what the child needs, then the child can conclude something must be wrong with it. Why else wouldn't they have helped? None of this is necessarily conscious. But if a baby or child learns that others won't help, they feel shame. The experience of shame becomes woven into their brain and their body.'

Research shows that if a parent doesn't notice, share or respond to a baby's emotions, it can become overwhelming for the baby's central nervous system. In the powerful and widely replicated 'Still-face' experiment, babies are seen to become terribly distressed when a parent stops engaging and presents the baby with a blank or 'still' face, having just been playing with them. Developmental psychologists suggest that our baby's central nervous system is still too 'fragile' to handle the confusion and discomfort they feel in being 'ignored' by the parent. It tells us something about the power of our relationship with our babies! If you are able, do take a look at the videos I reference on page 293 and you will see how the babies in the study use all manner of means to draw their parents' attention back to them – vocalising and even waving or banging their fists, then heartbreakingly turning away, with a hopeless expression on their faces when they fail. Then miserable tears start to fall. Our babies thrive on our interactions with them and I think this information can help us to be more aware when using our mobile phones or screens in front of our children, especially our babies, because more recent studies have replicated the same findings with parents using mobile phones rather than just a still face.

In realising that our children can experience a real sense of powerlessness if we ignore their attempts to engage with us, we can hopefully manage our time on our phones and screens to ensure they are never left feeling we love our phones more than them! It does not mean to say we should not use them, or indeed feel guilty when we do. We live in a modern world where home working is often a necessity and our own connectedness to the outside world – especially as a new parent – will often depend on us having our phones nearby. This is understandable, just as long as when our babies (in fact our children at any age) let us know they need our attention, that we shift our gaze to them. In being responsive parents, by picking up on our babies' cues, knowing that they may FEEL rejected if we are gazing at a screen rather than them, then we can more readily respond if they cry. Our babies thrive on our interactions with them and they need us to help them manage the sensations they will feel in their bodies. Unlike older children and adults, babies are developmentally unable to regulate their emotional states. We need to help them do it. In picking them up in these moments, in holding them close to our bodies, we can help them to regulate again and, in doing so, we have the opportunity to actually strengthen our connection with them. This is where trust is formed between us and our children – again 'when I need Mum/Dad, I can trust that they will be there for me'. All the things we discussed in Chapters 1 and 2 that keep that little lizard and baboon feeling safe and secure.

According to Dr Zeedyk: 'When we realise babies can feel [emotions] we realise how important relationships are to their development, then we get better at giving [children] the kind of care that makes parents feel proud of themselves for offering.'

I think this could go for considering not just our actions when we are around our children but what we buy in these early years too. Prams, for instance. When we understand that every minute of every day, our baby's experience shapes their brain, we might consider buying one that faces us so that when we walk, we can talk to our children more. According to fascinating research from New Zealand, this helps with language development. For them to read even our tiny facial expressions as we talk, builds up that healthy brain architecture, allowing us to readily reassure them if we are in a noisy street with lorries charging by, or if a dog barks loudly next to them.

The overriding point here is that our babies and children feel emotions VERY INTENSELY, they create huge spikes of feelings. Incredibly, modern science actually now enables us to SEE these emotions as they are experienced *inside our brains*. For example, we can see the 'pain' a child experiences in their brain when they watch Mum kiss their newborn sibling's head! We can also see the positive neural connections that are made when the newborn *feels* that kiss. Science shows us now how these everyday interactions are felt inside our children's brains ... and their bodies, as we know from Chapter 2.

Without emotional regulation, our children can very quickly become overwhelmed. Let me give you one final example that illustrates the accumulative effect of multiple emotions and also why we simply have to help our children regulate them. Imagine a little girl who is invited to a party, her best friend is four and everyone she knows at pre-school is going. There will be cakes, music, games and lots and lots of FUN!

However, the day before the party, she develops a fever and has to stay away from the party.

To this little girl, the sense of disappointment will be ENORMOUS. As Dr Zeedyk says, this comes out of the failure of hope. 'You are looking forward to something, you are excited, and BOOM!, it doesn't happen. Coping with that loss of hope is hard. Sometimes it sends children "into overwhelm" and they have a meltdown. That's what we often see in toddlers' tantrums. They can't cope with the mix of emotions – disappointment, frustration, betrayal, loss. All at the same time! Their body is experiencing so many different emotions all at once that it just kind of implodes. We tend to focus only on the behaviour, because that's what our culture has taught us to do. But underneath that behaviour are lots of tough, clashing emotions.'

When we understand how tough it is for our children to handle their big emotions without a wise owl to step in, then we can be SO much more sympathetic! Understanding our children's emotions can help us to parent with compassion, calmness and curiosity, keen to understand what might be going on for our children in these moments, where once we might have assumed they were just being 'naughty', now we know differently!

There's no such thing as 'naughty', remember?

So, given how INTENSE, COMPLEX and VARIED our emotions can be, what can we do as parents to help our children learn this vital capacity of emotional regulation? We want our children to become 'emotionally literate', or 'emotionally competent', as one of my esteemed colleagues, Dr Gabor Maté, calls it. We can do that when we help them understand what their emotions are and how they might make them feel.

TOOL KIT TIP

Naming emotions with your child

When my son was younger, he went through a period of not wanting to watch any movies that had sad music in them. When I asked him why, he said, 'Because I might cry.' Apparently, he had cried at a piece of music in school assembly ('Puff the Magic Dragon' which, when I listened to it again as an adult, agreed it IS actually a rather sad song which talks of loss and grief!). In that assembly, when he cried, someone had said something derogatory, so now he thought it was wrong to cry. He was only just four.

When you sense your child is having difficulty, they are angry, sad, joyful, excited and so on, we can name the emotion so they know what they feel has a 'name', that it's an actual *thing*, i.e., that it's normal.

So I asked, 'Wilbur, what is it that you feel when you hear the music?'

'Sad.'

'Well, it's okay to be sad. It is normal to be sad – it's actually a rather sad song! We all get sad sometimes. And it's okay to show that we are sad. It's normal.'

'Let's think about what we do when we are happy.' I then asked him.

'We laugh,' he said, looking up at me.

'And how might we show we are sad?'

'We cry.'

Getting our children used to the concept of having emotions by naming them will be enormously helpful. Wilbur didn't really know why that music made him cry at school, but once that was explained, in the future he will not be so surprised or uncomfortable if it happens again. He can understand our body's response to emotions: we laugh, we cry, we might shiver if we are scared or think we need the loo. We can explain to our children how the body's stress response works using the very simple concept of the lizard, baboon and the wise owl. Just giving your young child this knowledge will help make them feel much more in control of those feelings, not ashamed of them.

Also, crucially, your child needs to know that ALL emotions are valid, despite what Grandma might have told you. For example, it is absolutely okay to be angry if someone crosses a line with us – if someone wrongs us, abuses our trust, or lashes out physically and hurts us. Anger is a valid emotion that tells us we have been wronged. In responding, we can either behave like the surgeon with the scalpel and rant and rave at those around us, threatening harm because we can't express ourselves safely, or we can use our words, which is precisely what we are going to teach our children to do.

As we saw in Chapter 2, our children cry or flail around because they can't articulate what they are feeling, because these emotions feel VERY BIG in their body and they don't know what it is that they are feeling. However, once they know the NAMES of emotions, and they can tell you they feel sad or happy or angry, in that moment you will have both made HUGE leaps towards creating their own self-sufficient wise owl brain. They will begin to understand the highs and lows of their emotions as they arise. When they understand there is a name for what they are feeling, they can understand it is not 'wrong' to feel the way they do. Once that happens those tears will become fewer and further between.

When you help your child to be 'in touch' with, and recognise, their feelings, believe me, they'll be the one leading their team collaboratively and successfully, because you have helped equip them in these first five years with a strong emotional foundation and their own, fully functioning wise owl brain!

Now let's look at how to DEAL with the BIG feelings that can trigger a baboon stress response and create the most frequent and BIGGEST physical outcomes – the meltdowns and angry outbursts as our children try to get rid of the stress that they are left with inside.

For this one we need to bring in the SAS!

TOOL KIT TIP

SAS Parenting

When our children's lizards are leaping and their baboons are on the rampage, when those emotions are running riot and stress hormones are surging through their body, we need to step in, SAS-style. No, I don't mean RAMBO it with camouflage and a gun slung over your shoulder, but you do need to go in fast and targeted.

We can be true HEROES to our children, not by buying them big gifts at Christmas, but rather by being 'brave' enough to sit with them when they have been hijacked by their BIG feelings.

This is the key to their emotional regulation. To do this, we need SAS Parenting:

- **S**ay what you *see*
- **A**cknowledge
- **S**oothe

Let me explain: with my husband Mike being a former Royal Marines commando, he is the perfect person to illustrate **SAS Parenting**!

Mike once came inside the house exasperated because three-year-old Clemency had cried that after he had parked the car, he had 'got out the wrong way' and needed him to do it again, but on her side.

'Bloody hell, it's like being held hostage!' he said, frustrated. Trying to suppress my smile, I asked him how he had reacted.

Laughing he said, 'I had your voice in my head. You would say, "However ridiculous, there must be a reason for this," so I simply did as she asked!'

Clearly it made little sense to him (or anyone watching him walking around the parked car to get in and out again!) but he felt secure and confident enough in my theories to keep it simple and follow her lead. He knew he could STOP SN-O-T that this was not about him, rather there was something going on for Clemency.

On reflection later, we each suspected her need to have Daddy do as she had asked had its roots in sibling jealousy given her little brother Wilbur had been sitting 'behind Daddy' for the whole journey beforehand and she wanted Mike to now do something 'on her side'.

It might sound ridiculous to us as adults with all the perspective of our wise owls, but to a little baboon at three years old, the feeling of jealousy is VERY real. (Remember, jealousy is the subsidiary emotion, born out of fear and anger, combined from the concern that the baby might take away Mummy and Daddy's attention.)

In these moments, we can use STOP S'NOT and then deploy our SAS Parenting ... in essence it simply means we attune to our children – meet them at whatever state of arousal they are at and bring them down gently. In fact, much like a hostage negotiator would.

1 Say what you *see*

When we say what we *see*, this allows our child to feel SEEN and HEARD, which in turn will help to calm the baboon and lizard. When they are calm and feel connected to us, we can literally and metaphorically take them by the hand and move forward.

We can NAME the emotion if we suspect we know what it is. Don't use it negatively though – ALL our emotions are valid.

Use age-appropriate language; as few words as possible, keep it simple and keep it calm. You are going in SAS-style, remember. And if you are only in earshot at that moment, you can say what you are hearing.

So, for example . . .

'Clemency, Daddy can see you are really, really CROSS!'

Or 'Gosh, Clemency, you seem so ANGRY!'

Say this with a sing-song voice, your volume matching theirs, but not in an aggressive way. We want to attune to the baboon but not make him feel even more cross and threatened!

SAYING WHAT WE SEE allows our children to know that what they are feeling is REAL and that we understand it and are not dismissing them in this moment. We are validating their big feeling, because it IS valid (even if it might not appear to be in that moment!).

Then

2 Acknowledge

You are going to acknowledge what it is you think they need or want. Again, this helps the baboon know it is being understood and will also encourage their fluffy owlet to step in.

'You want Daddy here?'

Keep the words brief and keep eye contact. Your face should be calm and, with a look of concern, you are telling the baboon you really do want to help. You are SAS remember – this is a delicate negotiation.

At this point Clemency is highly likely to nod through her tears. Mike can go round the car to where she wants him to be. In these moments, we can even find the humour and enjoy our success in bringing our little baboons back down to 'earth' again.

3 Soothe

This is where you get to 'rescue' your child in this moment. You get to feel like Rambo but without the carnage. You have rescued your child from their too big and too painful emotions – get you, you Special Forces parent, you!

'Okay, darling, Daddy is here.'

Or, perhaps, 'Oh, little one, come here, let Daddy help you.'

When we have rescued our child and scooped them up in our arms and used appropriate and calming, soothing language, we are helping to bring them 'back to balance', because we know that with our physical contact and our wise owl words, we will see those anti-anxiety chemicals flooding through our children, calming them down, with all the feel-good hormones like oxytocin that make our children fall in love with us all over again.

HUGS must never be underestimated, because CUDDLES ARE KING! (or queen!), literally building strong neural pathways in your child's brain and creating positive memories that go into the baboon's memory sack as he registers that Dad is really cool, he really 'gets' me and 'understands'.

In this moment, what Mike has done is meet our daughter in her distress and he has met her pain with compassion. Instead of seeing Clemency as 'naughty', he sees that she has a need, in this instance a need to feel more secure within the family unit after a new baby brother has arrived. By using SAS parenting, he ensures that she is not left with those painful feelings all by herself.

Mike reflects on the episode this way:

   Man-ouevres with Mike

'I saw a cartoon a few years ago that resonated with me. It showed a dishevelled, obviously frustrated parent exasperatingly telling her child that, "Your attitude is seriously affecting how I wanted to be a parent!" I still show it to friends now. It's a great reminder that our children won't always behave how we think or want them to. A toddler trying to climb out of a pram to walk or having a meltdown about you getting out the "wrong side of the car" might seem a total pain in the backside, but if we step back and look at it from their baboon's perspective, we realise it's *our* projection on *them* – we push our views on them. Why, when we can go with the flow and get out the other side or enjoy a slower but fun and sunny walk home together? I take that as a win–win now, whereas before I might have gone into battle, seeing it as a threat to my authority. I appreciate it's a generalisation but, speaking anecdotally and, indeed, personally, I think fathers might fear if you give in to emotional demands now that we will lose control of our children later. In following Kate's example, I realise now precisely the opposite to be true. I now understand that it's not about that at all.'

Gawd, love my hubby! I'd agree of course! What this is about comes back to our EMOTIONS. In responding to Clemency with compassion and understanding, Mike was actually helping her to become emotionally secure. At this young age, her jealousy (as I will discuss in Chapter 12 on sibling rivalry) was borne out of an unconscious fear . . . that her baby brother is loved more than her. This fear is very real to that lizard and baboon – they know from thousands of years of evolution that being abandoned could mean death. Clemency was 'testing' Mike, yes, albeit in an unconscious way, testing that he loved her as much as Wilbur and therefore would not abandon her.

Let's look at another example, this time it's one that comes from happiness. It's pretty obvious how this emotion feels inside us, right? Gorgeous, delicious, warm emotions that make us feel really, really good! So good, in fact, that we might end up making like Tom Cruise bouncing on Oprah's sofa. Well, happiness can feel incredible when we are not 'afraid' of how big it feels inside. But it will seem REALLY BIG to our children because it is another 'heightened state of arousal' that will be felt intensely in their bodies. We WANT our children to experience the heights of joy, because life can be lived in true multi-colour when they can. But it is worth remembering that in our young children, with only a fluffy owlet to calm things down, they need our help here with happiness as much as with sadness, anger or other more obviously overwhelming emotions – put simply, their happiness might feel *too much* to contain!

> **Brain Box**
>
> 'Joy is a bodily state. To feel heights of joy as opposed to just pleasure we have to be moved from the very depths of us. Joy is the result of human connection. By and large those ➡

who live their lives to the fullest, are likely to have been parented in ways that have repeatedly activated intense positive brain chemical and bodily arousal states.'

Psychotherapist Dr Margot Sunderland, *The Science of Parenting*

We want our children to experience joy, but as one of those big emotions we want to help them do so without them becoming overwhelmed.

Imagine your two young children are playing in another room building magnetic towers together. You can hear they are having a great time, at first, but pretty soon the sounds coming from next door begin to get increasingly excited. The game has become so exciting that they are in danger of a 'joy overload'. You suddenly hear howls rather than laughter. It might just be that your younger ones have ticked over into 'overload', and that they have become overstimulated and you are now needed to intervene and calm things down again. When overexcitement happens, it all becomes 'a bit much' and the joy can all too easily tip over into something else.

Well, once again, we use SAS Parenting.

1 Say what you *see*

With your voice at a similar volume, a smile on your face and perhaps a whoop to match theirs, you will attune to your children, which feels GOOD to them – and it should feel good to you, too!

'WOW! That's incredible! What an amazing tower you have both built! I can *see* how EXCITED [the emotion] you are to have built that!'

We don't want our children to stop feeling the joy inside them, we want to be able to meet them in their joy and to encourage it so that they learn this is also an okay BIG feeling to have! This is a feeling that is safe, even when they are so excited that they literally don't know what to do with themselves! In doing this, we help our children experience joy fully and not see them repress this wonderful feeling of arousal later on in life.

Once we have 'met' them in their heightened state, we then can gently bring them back down again before it tips into them being overwhelmed. This is what helps them to build their own emotional regulation. So, next up we . . .

2 Acknowledge

'It must feel really GOOD to have built it SO so high! I can SEE everyone has been having SO much fun! But it sounds like someone is getting a bit upset/sad, do you need me to come and help?'

Then . . .

3 Soothe

'Come, shall Mummy join you, so we can all play together?'

In this instance, **soothing** again is about 'matching' them as they play and, in their delight, whooping alongside them when it feels warranted and mirroring their body language and tone of voice when you want to help them come 'back down' again.

Here are a few more examples of questions we might ask our children in the 'moment' if it feels like they are having a tough time with their emotions, or if they are a little older and raise something that is troubling them:

- Gosh, I can see how upset you are.'
- 'Can you tell me how it feels inside?'
- 'You seem a little sad.'
- 'I can see how cross you are.'
- 'You seem rather angry, can you tell me what's going on?'
- 'That sounds difficult.'
- 'It seems quite hard for you, right now.'
- 'Maybe it feels difficult to know what to do.'

It often helps to pause, as they will sometimes 'fill the gaps . . .' Often, nothing more is needed here other than you being present for your child and them feeling that you really are interested in what they have to say.

And, remember, if there is resistance it's okay – it's not personal – you can follow up with:

'Mummy/Daddy wants to help.'

These are just a few examples of the types of questions that will allow your child to sense that you UNDERSTAND they are having a tough time of it EMOTIONALLY.

When we are SAS parents, rather than turning away and leaving our children alone with *their* big feelings, we can instead head towards them, knowing we can help them sit with their big feelings. SAS Parenting will help you show your youngster that you SEE them in their emotional distress, that you not only understand it, but you are not afraid of it, which will then help them to not be afraid of *their* 'too big emotions'.

When you are an SAS parent, you can stare down those who might say children should 'suck it up', or 'Oh, look, here come the waterworks,' or 'stop being a drama queen!'

As an SAS parent, you have the insight to know that suppressing your child's emotions like this can only end one way: with a massive EXPLOSION of emotion. It's of NO BENEFIT; in fact, it is a startling negative. They might grow into adults forced to carry a lifetime of emotional baggage, a heavy rucksack on their back, with them stuffing in those rocks of upset as they go.

Instead, we want to create future adults who have robust, healthy emotional regulation that will mean they are ready for whatever life throws at them.

And if there's room for any further convincing, might I ask the question: who would you rather have operating on YOU? The surgeon with a calm, measured, balanced wise owl brain . . . or the raging baboon with a scalpel in his hand?!

Wise Owl Wisdoms

ᴠ ᴠ   Emotions have their roots in evolution and are designed as part of a survival mechanism. They are valid and can be managed when we understand how and why they drive our behaviour.

ᴠ ᴠ   We must help our children understand what emotions are and how they might be felt in the body – we can do this by talking to our children about how they are feeling and then NAMING the emotions.

ᴠ ᴠ   Our children won't always know themselves why they are behaving as they do, which is why often just soothing and saying you understand can be enough.

ᴠ ᴠ   **SAS Parenting** helps us teach our children to regulate their emotions. When we say what we see, acknowledge their upset then soothe any emotional pain, we will meet our children in whatever emotion they feel and help bring our children down gently again.

Let's put it this way: when it comes to our children in their emotional distress, who would you rather be: *the HERO heading INTO the fray to help them with their big feelings, or the parent running away, leaving them to manage all alone?*

CHAPTER 5

Crying as Communication

'Crying is never a symbol of weakness.
From the time we are born, it has
always been a sign that we are alive.'

ANON

Our children cry for a reason – babies especially, given it is pretty much their only way of conveying to us what it is they need. Clearly, given babies can't move their arms or legs to flee or fight, they have to use their voice instead. Mother Nature designed a baby's screams to be as loud and urgent as a car alarm to make sure we respond! Some studies have measured babies' cries at around the 100–120 decibel (dB) mark – normal conversation is 50dB, a rock concert is 120dB and a nearby jet plane is 150dB – so your baby can cry pretty loudly!

When a baby cries, it is essentially telling us, 'Mum/Dad ... I need you.' No mammal will ignore a crying cub, because a baby's cries are a call for help: for food, water, comfort, protection, and so on – all the things they need to survive.

Our babies cry when they need us; our young children do the same.

When we understand that our children's distress is felt in their bodies, as we saw in Chapter 2, we can help to soothe and calm them down, responding to their needs, whether that is to change a nappy or kiss a scraped knee. MRI scans actually show how this builds those all-important connections in our children's brains.

This is why I say cuddles are king (or queen!). When we cuddle our young children when they are crying, feel-good hormones are released in their brains, too, the opioids and oxytocin – the so-called 'love drugs'. We want as much of this in their early years as we can!

> **Brain Box**
>
> 'If you consistently soothe your child's distress over the years and take any anguished crying seriously, highly effective response systems can be established in his brain. These will help him to cope well with stress later in life.'
>
> Psychotherapist Dr Margot Sunderland, *The Science of Parenting*

It is sometimes asserted that babies cannot 'remember' their earliest experiences, but the work of the eminent psychiatrist Dr Bruce Perry and his colleagues at the Child Trauma Academy in the United States, as well as the work of the distinguished psychologist and leading memory specialist, Professor Daniel Schacter, reveal that while we may not *consciously* recall what we learned in our first years, we do in fact have 'emotional' memories that may last a lifetime. In the book *Splintered Reflections*, Dr Perry explains to the authors that even though a child might not be able to articulate a certain memory, it does not mean they have not 'stored' the experience. For example, if we were frightened as a baby by a large dog lunging and barking at the pram it may influence how we react upon hearing a dog barking later in life. From the research I have done it seems that our unconscious memories can very much influence how we perceive the world and how we react to situations later in life.

> *Brain Box*
>
> 'The first year establishes our deepest sense of who we are, the strength and solidity of our identity. Between six months and three years, the responsiveness of our parents and the consistency of the care we receive affects how emotionally secure we are in relationships.'
>
> Child clinical psychologist Oliver James, author of *How to Develop Emotional Health*

Sleep and crying

We currently live in a much more time-pressured world, which I fear has led us more often to have to try to fit our babies and children into OUR schedules, forcing them to adapt to *our* needs, rather than serving THEIRS. I say this again as a working mum, having felt those same pressures myself. However, when we look to traditional communities, we are reminded of how distanced we have become from our children's natural needs: to be close to us, to be held by us, to be seen and heard. When our babies cry in the night, they are not doing it to be 'difficult' (although I can appreciate it might feel like that when we have a 6am start and a hundred emails to answer).

Of course, the reality is there is no 'quick fix'.

These early years can be difficult. It is here that parents need the most support. In tribal communities, new mothers will have had that support from other families around them. Sadly, today, this happens less often, leading to practices where a baby is left to 'cry it out' and left unsoothed over a prolonged period.

I have heard it said, 'Oh, but it's okay to leave the baby to cry itself out', or 'that baby is wrapping you around its finger', or even, 'It's fine to go away for a week without them; they don't remember.'

But the scientists I have interviewed tell us otherwise.

Renowned psychotherapist Dr Margot Sunderland told me that, 'One of the biggest problems in the past has been the assumption that the child's developing brain is a robust structure that can withstand all manner of stress. Neuroscientific research has now found this to be a fallacy. Whilst children have some measure of resilience and – genetically speaking some more than others – the developing brain in those crucial first years of life is also highly vulnerable to stress. It is so sensitive that the stress of many common parenting techniques can alter delicate "emotion chemicals".'

I interviewed Dr Bruce D. Perry, American psychiatrist and senior fellow of the Child Trauma Academy in Houston, Texas on this subject. His work in this field is hugely acclaimed. When discussing the impact of prolonged crying, he told me that, 'There has been a popular perspective that allows a parent to engage in a practice that may lead to a child crying less at night, but they don't understand that's only a pattern of stress activation that is going to make their child less resilient over time and, in fact, for some children, may actually make them more sensitised and dysregulated. It really is having the exact opposite effect of what they want in the long run.'

Generally, our children will be more settled and cry less when they feel safe and their needs are met.

> **Brain Box**
>
> 'An uncomforted child will stop crying eventually if there is no response. But there are real costs. We are not talking about a parent rushing to a baby who cries as soon as her bottom lip starts to wobble ... prolonged crying is the crying that anyone sensitive to the pain of others will recognise as a desperate calling for help. It is the type of crying that goes on and on and eventually stops when the child is either completely exhausted and falls asleep or in a hopeless state realises that help is not going to come. Stress from prolonged crying and separations can affect a baby's developing brain and it can affect the brain for life.'
>
> Psychotherapist Dr Margot Sunderland, *The Science of Parenting*

I can appreciate this information can be difficult to read if you are a parent to children who are a little older and you did leave your child to 'cry it out' when they were young, because this was often the advice in the past. However, the science now allows us to see this differently. Where we once might not have known it – we do now. And you deserve to know, because I appreciate these are difficult decisions to take. If it does feel difficult, please take heart, the information you now have can be used to great benefit for you and your child. When we respond to our babies if they cry, and dry our toddlers' tears, we are building those all-important healthy connections in their brain, strengthening the bond we share and the 'secure attachment' we want our children to have with us.

Addiction specialist and physician Dr Gabor Maté agrees. 'Few parents want to leave their children alone with their tears and yet in our stressed-out society we may often be told, "your baby is controlling your life". The best interest of a baby is often not the most convenient to the parents. It is natural for infants to cry at night, and it is in the maternal instinct to respond sensitively to their needs, even if that means many sleepless nights and a constant state of fatigue. No caring parent would risk the health of a child by seeking advice from unqualified medical practitioners. Parents should therefore be wary of blindly following the guidance of sleep trainers with no credentials that could put the mental well-being of their children at risk.'

Gabor Maté explains the risk in this way: 'When an infant falls asleep after a period of wailing and frustrated cries for help, it is not that she has learned the "skill" of falling asleep. What has happened is that her brain, to escape the overwhelming pain of abandonment, shuts down. It's an automatic neurological mechanism. In effect, the baby gives up. The short-term goal of the exhausted parents has been achieved, but at the price of harming the child's long-term emotional vulnerability. Encoded in her cortex is an implicit sense of a non-caring universe.'

In psychotherapy, we learn that 'we can always repair' and when we commit to invest in emotional regulation with our children in these early years, we can help them enormously and – as we know – there will be plenty of opportunities to do that!

When we respond to our babies if they cry, and dry our toddlers' tears, we are reassuring them that we can be trusted and will always be there to help them feel safe. It is this that builds the healthy connections in our children's brains, making them more emotionally healthy.

There are numerous resources that I have listed in the references to this book to support these findings, and I share them because it's such an important and often divisive topic. I can only share with you what my husband and I did as parents, having researched the topic in exhaustive depth. This was the route we decided was best for our children, based on the science that I had read, extracts of which I have mentioned above. It worked for my family; it is up to you to decide what will work for yours.

I understand the first few years can be terribly fraught. I remember those early days all too well with my own children when they were babies. I remember the sleepless nights and the absolute confusion that having a crying child can cause, triggering our own baboons and lizards to do somersaults with the stress of it all.

At one point, when Clemency was a newborn, my ever-practical husband gently suggested we put up a list of the main things Clemency needed when I was run ragged and wild-eyed as she cried.

Hungry
Thirsty
Overtired
Needs a nappy change
Cold
Hot
In pain

I learned that when once I had sorted those, then the one remaining thing I could do was COMFORT her . . . I accepted that if I had ticked off that list, I knew what she needed was me to help soothe her. I discovered that she loved being held in a sling on my chest, with me doing what I now call the '**Happy Hippo Hug**', where I would slowly bend at the knees, and come up again, making soothing hippo sounds (you might need to google that one!) as I did. The low grunts in her ear worked to soothe her and the motion of my body helped calm her down.

The principle of why this might have worked for me can be found in the work of Dr Bruce Perry again. He explained to me that the way to help ourselves and our babies and young children to move from a 'super-high anxiety state' to a calmer state is *rhythm*. He says tribal cultures have known this for thousands of years, with singing, dancing and drumming being a mainstay to bring the tribe together, especially as a healing process.

Dr Perry describes this as, 'patterned, repetitive rhythmic activity using brain stem-related somatosensory networks which make your brain accessible to relational (limbic brain) reward and cortical thinking'.

Again, with the theme of keeping this simple, this scientific explanation actually brings us back to our lizard and baboon again. Our babies were regulated in the womb, when their lizard brain was in charge. Anything that helps keep the lizard feeling safe and secure will help to recreate in some form that sense of being regulated and well whilst in the womb, when everything was 'taken care of': the baby was fed, at the right body temperature, could hear the comforting beat of mum's heart, and so on. It is why our babies often respond well to us going for a walk with them. (Perhaps in the pram, but better still if we carry them in a sling or papoose on our chest. When we sing or hum, so much the better!)

You will find out what works for you and your baby by trial and error. The elements that most often work will include turning down the lights, ensuring your baby is not too hot or too cold, being close to you (skin on skin when they are very young), gentle movement, rocking, anything that may mimic the environment of the womb. And anything that helps them to feel 'safe'. This is what is key. When the lizard feels 'safe', your baby/toddler will feel calm. At night, clearly our children, if they are sleeping in their own rooms, might tend to feel less 'safe' because their ancient 'primitive' brain does not register that you are only sleeping in the next room; they just know it is dark and they are alone. There were nights when my husband said he felt like a bomb-disposal expert, tiptoeing out of the nursery, frightened of stepping on the one squeaky floorboard that would see Clemency up and howling again. As a result, we ended up co-sleeping with our children. Again, this was our personal decision, based on what worked for us as a family and the research we had done. This is for you to decide, based on the medical and professional advice you are given. (Again, I list references and resources at the back of the book, if you would like to learn more.) I know some parents will also worry that once we allow our children into bed with us it will always be the case.

I can only say in that regard that I found my children quite naturally progressed to then sleeping in their own bedrooms. Clemency was around three when she slept all night in her own bed and Wilbur was four. And, yes, that may have had you spitting out your tea (FOUR?!), but I figured I would let them find their way and sleeping in the same bed was easier than keep getting up in the night. They both now happily sleep through the night and in their own bedrooms.

When we attend to our children's needs, we help them to regulate and ultimately soothe themselves; when we do that, they will sleep more soundly and you can rest assured. But if our children are in distress – and, by that, I mean crying that tells us they are in pain, emotionally or physically – I *always* respond. Think about the lizard again: if the baby is alone in the dark at night and there's a loud noise, the little lizard might panic that a predator is nearby and fear that it will be eaten. As I explained in Chapter 2, the metaphorical lizard might scamper up the baobab and ask the baboon for help. The baboon may press the 'fire alarm' (the amygdala) to sound the warning. In their physical reality, our babies being afraid will trigger those stress hormones and see a cortisol surge in the body. They then need us to help them calm down.

When we can be our child's wise owl, helping them to regulate their emotions, we help calm the lizard and the baboon so they work as they should, and in time help our children grow a wise owl of their own so they are able to soothe themselves and see *fewer* tears in the future.

I must emphasise that you really must do what you feel will work for you – perhaps the message is to ensure you get to the root cause of any upset – if we always remember that if our children are crying *they have a need*. This goes for our toddlers and five-year-olds as much as our five-month-olds. I found an old proverb recently that said, 'What soap is to the body, tears are for the soul', and from my perspective, in these first five years, if your children are crying, it should simply be seen as communication. Tears tell us that our children are in 'distress' and, remember, I see tears as 'stress leaving the body', and, having read Chapter 2, you will understand why stress leaving the body is actually a very good thing to encourage! For our older children we can again soothe them with our words, using a low voice, soft tones and simple language. We can still use that rhythm with our older children, too, rocking them, singing to them, going for a walk, all things that can help to restore that little lizard and baboon back to calm.

If they are really distressed, you know you can also deploy SAS Parenting:

Say what you see, acknowledge the upset, soothe the pain.

- **Say**: 'Oh, sweetheart, I can *see* you are REALLY upset.'
- **Acknowledge**: 'You must have some really big feelings going on there.'
- **Soothe**: 'Come, can Mummy/Daddy help?'

You don't need to say too much more or be too specific when your children are distressed –they might not be able to 'hear' you very well given their lizard brain can sometimes have them 'emotionally freeze' (ultimately, that is often the only response they have at their disposal, given fight–flight might not be possible). Your empathy at these times will be enough and may even see your child cry a little harder. That's a good sign, because it means they have a lot to release and now you are offering a safe space for them to release it.

As we said when talking about STOP S'Not, be aware of your own body language, keep down low, open your arms, look genuinely sympathetic (even sometimes when the tears might be over something ostensibly comical – like the bread being the wrong 'colour'). It might not be about the 'bread', remember, you cannot always know for sure, but one thing you *can* know is that you can be the wise owl for your children in these moments, and when you put your 'wings' around them, you are not only repairing their hurt, you are building a bond for life.

When you are solo-parenting especially, these early years are TOUGH. Mike was once told that being a single parent was as stressful as being a fighter pilot in combat. (It is so important that you don't feel alone and I will look at this in more detail in Chapter 14.)

 Man-ouevres with Mike

'When they are young and you really want them to get to sleep, it can see you singing them lullabies and then leopard-crawling out of their bedroom like a member of Special Ops Seal Team 6. The fact is, you have to constantly remind yourself that their view of the world is different from ours and the physiology is different; thoughtful persuasion is normally the more powerful tool, even if sometimes you need a brain like chess legend Gary Kasparov to succeed. The motto of the Marines SBS (Special Boat Squadron) is, "By strength and guile", which pretty much sums up my parenting now they're a bit older!'

It might feel like a thankless task. But, hand on heart, it will be the best investment you ever make.

Wise Owl Wisdoms

- Crying is communication.
- How we respond to our children's cries now can influence how they see the world later.
- Comforting a child does not create a crybaby, rather the reverse.

CHAPTER 6

Star Jumps, Stress and the 'Salsa Shimmy'

'One thing I had learned from watching chimpanzees with their infants is that having a child should be fun.'

DR JANE GOODALL DBE,
primatologist and anthropologist

As we have seen from Chapter 2, we all experience stress to varying degrees in our lives – but, for a moment, imagine the stress felt by an impala on the vast, dry savannah, an expansive landscape with few hiding places and all too many predators. American clinical psychologist Peter Levine observed that when an impala is hunted by a lion – an almost constant threat – its stress response would obviously go into overdrive. As with humans, cortisol is released in massive doses to help the impala's body manage the stress and increase the blood sugar to fuel the muscles to make its escape.

Sometimes the impala will outrun the lion; other times it would do what the lizard did in Part 1 of this book, and simply drop to the floor, in that freeze or 'faint response' that could save its life, as few predators want to eat something that is already 'dead'.

Whatever evasive action was taken, Levine observed that after the chase the impala would stand up and shake uncontrollably for a few minutes, as though literally shaking out the stress of the terrifying last few minutes. Once that was done, the impala would simply go back to grazing again. Prey animals like deer or gazelles go through this physical process of shaking or trembling once the hunt is over and they have escaped. Levine concluded that the process of shaking is the animal's innate way of releasing the stress or the physical 'energy' of the event – that stress response we spoke about in Chapter 2. He reflected that in their instinctual way, these animals naturally release the trauma of the hunt from their bodies.

Further, Levine also observed that animals in the natural world don't experience post-traumatic stress. His life's work across multi-disciplines led him to create what he calls 'somatic experiencing', 'to release this stored energy, and turn off this threat alarm that causes severe dysregulation and dissociation'. This is, essentially, what the impala is doing after the threat has dissipated – discharging the stress that had just been suddenly generated in its body, in a controlled and safe way.

According to a number of similar studies, humans and zoo animals are the only mammals that <u>do not</u> do this. Aside from some traditional cultures we rarely go through this process. Somewhere along the way we appear to have 'unlearned' this healing behaviour.

What worked really well for us when we were living in caves, out on the hunt for food or running from sabre-toothed tigers, is not so great for our children. Often, our children are told to 'suck it up' or 'stop those tears'. This is a serious problem – if they repress that involuntary evolutionary reaction, our under-fives (and all children) are left with massive amounts of hormones coursing through their bloodstream with nowhere to go. As we saw in Chapter 2, stress will live in the body if it has no form of release. Prolonged or frequent stress in our children is clearly undesirable and can also be damaging to their vulnerable developing systems.

That is really not good. Not good at all. Remember, 'stress lives in the body'.

Let's step back from the scientific studies and think about the ways that our children CAN release stress naturally.

Our children might find stress release like the impala, even if, at first glance, it might not seem obvious to us, for example:

Jamilia is three and wants to walk along the wall on the way to pre-school.

Mum needs to get back on time for a call from her boss. Jamilia has been pulling her mum back – tugging, digging her heels in.

Tension builds and eventually Mum snaps. 'No! Come now, Jamilia we are late, we need to get to pre-school.'

Jamilia bursts into tears.

Mum is torn, compassionate for her daughter in her upset, but perhaps she doesn't want to seem weak by giving in.

'You want to walk the wall?'

Jamilia is still crying but nods her head.

'Okay, you can walk the wall ... but you must stop crying first.'

We might think we need to negotiate with our children so they don't become 'spoilt', that they must stop crying first otherwise they will always think they can get 'their own way'.

I understand that. Mike would certainly also understand this worry, after his 'hostage negotiations' with Clemency in the car. However, we need to understand that our very young children simply don't have the sophistication for this. Their genuine upset comes from a much more primitive place and happens when those stress hormones have built up and are then released in the only way they know how.

Tears on the way to school might be a sign of that stress. In this instance, it might suggest that Jamilia may already have been feeling overwhelmed (it's only her second day) and that her active baboon had seen a way to 'naturally release' some of that stress that was sitting in her body by climbing onto a wall and walking along it. Namely, getting rid of it with physical movement and doing something a little bit scary would help to counter the tension too!

So here we have a child doing something instinctive in response to something primitive – fear.

But Mum wants to negotiate. Mum wants her to 'stop crying first' in order to 'get her wish'. Mum wants Jamilia to understand that she cannot always cry to get what she wants.

But WHY?

Don't go into battle.

Put your Sherlock deerstalker hat on and ask yourself . . . the wall seems really important right now, I might not understand WHY in this moment but if it's so important, why not let her walk along it?

Go with Jamilia's response: recognise that her tears are a form of communication and that, right here and now, the wall is important to a little girl who might be using it for some form of release – and hey, yes, even if it brings her a little bit of joy, well, who would want to deny that, too?

'Ah!' I hear you say, 'but her mum is going to be late for her work call!'

Yes – that thing called modern life is encroaching on our relationships with our children once again. But this is too important to miss.

You know what? Walk the wall – your daughter will stop crying soon enough, not least when you can both laugh with glee at how 'brilliant' she is in doing so! What better outcome than to scoop her up on to there with a big smile, acknowledging, 'Ah! So, you wanted to walk the wall! Okay, Mummy understands.'

That's it.

Then enjoy the warm glow of a bond between you both, as your daughter walks the wall and heads into school feeling understood, loved and bonded.

No battles – no bother.

Okay, so I hear some people saying, 'Well, that's all well and good, but what if my boss fires me for being late?' Well, fair point, but all I would say is that if we are late because our children were in distress, then maybe review your morning routine for leaving the house and hopefully give yourself more time to get to work. If work starts at the same time every day, it is simple enough to allow a little more walking time and, to be fair to Jamilia, her episode probably lasted but a few brief minutes in total.

Over time, as your child realises and learns that you understand their stresses and can help them with their release, they will in return come to recognise the occasions when you REALLY do need to do something your way. They will comply far more readily because they have a bank of knowledge of when you worked with them, rather than dictating or imposing.

They will work *with* you because they will view you as a parent who usually says 'Yes', so when you do actually say no, they will more readily sense the need to work together. This is shaping and finessing their wise owl brain.

My children gave me the biggest compliment ever last week when I heard them say, 'Our mum is the best, she says YES ALL the time!' (Clearly, I don't! But I love that this is their perception and that's how they *FEEL*.)

*   *   *

Physical stress sits INSIDE our children's bodies when they have had a full-blown meltdown, are truly scared or on red alert for whatever reason. As we have just seen, crying can be accompanied by a need to physically release stress, which is when we see the whole-body reaction. We saw it with Wilbur – his whole body reacting as he released the 'stress' of his day at the wild nursery. But we also saw it in both our responses afterwards, when he and I had that natural inclination to roll around in the leaves ... which brings me to my next tool, which will help with stress control, and to explain this I need to take a lesson from the impala at the start of this chapter.

TOOL KIT TIP

Star Jumps and the Salsa Shimmy

One annual holiday we decided to go skiing – the first time for our kids. The children took to it quite naturally, a little giraffe-like at first, but they progressed really quickly. I stayed to watch both children over the first two mornings to ensure they were settled. I observed how many of the small children cried – not during the lesson itself, but when their parents came to collect them. This crying response was likely their way of releasing all the stress they had bottled up that morning after learning something new. They, like Wilbur at the wild nursery, had bottled up their emotions, only to let them all out when their safety net arrived in the form of their parents. It broke my heart a little to watch that some parents seemed uncomfortable with their child crying. No one is to blame here, because if we are parented that way ourselves, why would we think any differently? But now, when we understand this is just nature's way of releasing stress, we can comfort our children, confident that doing so will lead to less crying later in life, not more.

Later that week the children had made such good progress that Clemency was taken off to a different slope. I had seen her whizzing down the mountain with immense pride, watching her take the ski lift and out of my view again. However, a few hours later, a snowstorm hit and all hell broke loose. We could barely see beyond our hands. I skied down to where Wilbur had been collected by my husband, then I was back up the slopes to find my baby girl. I found her with the group, but she was in shock and in tears. Wrapping my arms around her, I guided her through the whiteout, back down the slopes to safety. This was more than about tears now though – I could see she was in shock.

'Clemency!' I said, trying to sound as bright as I could under the circumstances. 'I can see how scary that must have been.'

Deploy SAS Say what you see, acknowledge the upset, soothe those big feelings, use my calming presence.

Here, however, I could see that I needed to do more than just soothe. Clemency was in shock, her system flooded with cortisol and adrenaline.

I had recently been on *Strictly Come Dancing* and, drawing on that experience and my studies of experts such as Levine, and thinking back to the impala story, I had an idea: in my counselling training, my tutor Georgia always told us to 'shake it out' when we had finished an especially difficult session and I had been doing that, sometimes in the newsroom in between bulletins (I literally just stand up and "shake it all out"), or if I felt the need to simply get up and do some star jumps, or use my rebounder (small trampoline) after an especially long day.

I now call it the **Salsa Shimmy**.

I tried it with Clemency, 'Shall we try to shake it all out, darling? Let's just try. Let's do a 'Salsa Shimmy'!' For the next 30 seconds or so, my daughter and I stood in our skisuits, shimmying our butts and waving our arms like two red bears (think of Baloo in *The Jungle Book* when he scratches his back against the bark).

Within seconds we were laughing – she at me, and me at the wonderful relief of finding my daughter and bringing her back off the mountain.

We have used this idea so many times since. Sometimes we talk about being a 'jelly on a plate' (which is a song my mother used to sing when rubbing our hair dry after bath time), sometimes we call it the Pepper Pot Dance, sometimes we simply do star jumps. Each time injecting as much fun and humour as I can.

 It doesn't need to be salsa either! – running, walking, drumming, even knitting! It comes back to my conversation with Dr Bruce Perry. Our bodies know what to do instinctively. Just find a physical way to release those stress hormones and you will be following those natural instincts of our ancestors.

It doesn't matter what you want to call this, or however you want to frame it, just know that your child can literally shimmy that stress right out of their body! I must stress this is ONLY for a child who is able to stand independently and stomp their feet without our help.

Important We must NEVER shake or shimmy with babies or very young children. For our very young children, we can hold them close and do that slow and easy Happy Hippo!

Cuddles

Cuddles are a fantastic way of relieving stress at any age. When our children have been through a stressful experience, we can help them self-regulate by scooping them up with our big, wise owl wings and soothe away any residual stress.

These natural behaviours literally calm their lizard and ensure the stressful experience does not get stuck but is rather rocked out gently in our arms. When we return to our instincts and intuition as parents, we might realise that we quite naturally use a rhythmic motion when we cuddle our children, such as when you wrap them up after a bath and hold them in your arms and gently rock them back and forth – these are the times that healing will genuinely occur.

Your children might sometimes squirm if they are not used to you doing this, so don't force it! Offer your arms, those big owl wings, to wrap around them and soothe them, if you sense it might bring them comfort. When my children have been in distress in the past and are on overload, I often find myself simply whispering in their ear, 'It's okay, it's okay, it's okay', over and over for no other reason than it seems to soothe and comfort them. It would tie in perhaps with that sense of repetition and patterns that Dr Perry spoke about. Whatever feels natural and soothing will work.

Sometimes, if they are in a heightened state of anxiety, our children might be so overwhelmed they appear to not want us near them. That's okay too. Stay calm, remember **STOP**

SN-O-T – this is not about you. They are just overwhelmed. Sit with them in the room, **never** leave them in their distress, they are unable to do this alone. Sit with your back against a wall if you can, and resist the urge to 'do'.

Just let your child know you are there for them.

Find compassion for your child in that moment. They might be kicking at the bed, they might be shouting, screaming even. Recognise they are in full lizard/baboon mode, and in these moments it is okay not to even try to analyse why. **GO INTO SAS MODE** – say what you see, acknowledge they are finding something very tough, then soothe – and at all times, keep physically low so as not to loom large over them, keep your voice quiet and let them know you are not leaving.

Let them know you can *help*.

Our children will face hundreds of new experiences in these first five years, we need to recognise that expecting them to deal with stressful situations alone when they are young, then not helping them to 'discharge' that stress physically, might well see them develop into more nervous, anxious children instead. This is why I never send my children to their rooms if they are upset, which I will come to in Chapter 8.

 Man-ouevres with Mike

'My reflections on this chapter and particularly the skiing incident is that men, dare I say it, can sometimes focus on "solving the problem", rather than considering a child's emotional fallout. When things go wrong – as they inevitably will throughout our parenting journey – when we face an emergency as we did with the kids with the whiteout, it's worth considering how different people deal with emotional "fallout" differently. I remember collecting Wilbur who was also distressed by the whiteout, but my thoughts were instantly to berate *myself* for not buying him better gloves as he was so cold – and then I was angry about the judgement of the ski school who had taken them out! Kate's immediate thoughts were on the emotional fallout. Mine was on the practical. It didn't mean I wasn't caring, but I think sometimes we bury our own distress and upset, and perhaps gloss over the actual event, even perhaps playing down the situation, "Oh, you're all right now" because you want to put it in the past but, on reflection, that's not really so helpful!'

Wise Owl Wisdoms

ᵥ ᵛ Stress lives in the body.

ᵥ ᵛ In the natural world, animals will instinctively expel the energy of a stressful event.

ᵥ ᵛ Using Star Jumps and Salsa Shimmies, we can help our children do the same.

ᵥ ᵛ Where it is more age-appropriate, use the Happy Hippo Hug!

So my final WOW is:

ᵥ ᵛ When our children are on 'overload' (for whatever reason), simply staying with them while they 'work it out' is always a good thing!

CHAPTER 7

Father Christmas and the Code Red

*'I have always believed in the magic of
childhood and think that if you get it
right, the magic should never end.'*

COLIN THOMPSON,
children's author and illustrator

'Twas the night before Christmas (there is a book in there somewhere) ... I heard the most terrible commotion coming from
upstairs. I heard screaming from one child and my husband was
shouting. Never a good thing and especially unusual to hear from
Mike, who rarely raises his voice. I flew up the stairs and bumped
into my husband at the bathroom door.

'Christ Almighty, it's just impossible!' he shouted.

I could barely hear him above Wilbur, who was thrashing

around in the bath and screeching, 'I DON'T WANT TO GET OUT OF THE BATH!'

Water was everywhere and both father and son were clearly in distress. I took the bathrobe from my husband's hand and ran in to Wilbur.

'Sweetheart, what's wrong?!'

My husband stood behind me. 'He is refusing to get out of the bath!'

It had been 18 months since the wild nursery incident and the meltdowns had been much fewer and further between, so I knew something serious must have happened. However, at the moment, I could not see what. I could see the equivalent of a large looming caveman in the form of my husband, standing over a cold, wet, soap-covered equivalent of a small chimpanzee.

My immediate thought was how best to bring the situation down a notch.

I knelt by the bath, looked into Wilbur's eyes and opened my arms.

But he threw himself backwards, wailing, 'Daddy's mean!'

I sensed 'Daddy' bristling behind me.

'Okay, Wilbur! You want stay in the bath?!'

Mike looked at me as though I had lost the plot. I had no intention of letting Wilbur stay in – I just wanted to connect with him before he fell and hurt himself. I tried to sound bright and breezy but my own brain was on red alert with the noise and nature of what was going on. After the wild nursery incident, I felt more confident that he would calm down if I could just find the connection. We had made enough progress in that 18 months to know this wasn't really about the bath – there was (as always) *something else* going on. I just couldn't tell what it was yet.

'Okay, Mummy understands.' (I didn't, really.)

'I want to get you out – it's cold.' (I could almost SEE Wilbur's fluffy owlet thinking that one through ... *Hmm, actually it IS quite cold!*)

'Let me help you.'

Typically, Wilbur would now open his arms and throw them around my neck with the offer of me helping, but tonight was different. His eyes were wide, seeing me, but not yet able to calm down.

'Okay,' I said a little more firmly, 'Mummy is going to get you out so you don't hurt yourself.'

'No!' He cried, 'Daddy's mean!'

With that he pushed me away.

Clearly, he still felt misunderstood – or something ...

He held up a fist as though to hit me and I flinched.

'Wilbur, that's not okay.' My voice was still gentle but firm now. I laid the boundary. 'We don't hit, sweetheart, however mad we are.'

Shaking my head, we made eye contact. He had heard my words but he was still on edge, body tense and fists clenched. With water all over the bathroom floor, I was still worried he would hurt himself if he slipped, so in haste I tried again.

'Wilbur, let Mummy help you. Tell me what's wrong.'

Something clicked.

His body relaxed and I took my chance. I scooped him up out of the bath and wrapped a white towelling robe around him. I had him safely then and relaxed for the first time, drawing his little body into mine, sitting back on the tiled floor with my back against the bathroom door. I held him and said, 'It's okay, it's okay,' over and over, rocking him as I whispered it.

Then came the sobs. His whole body shook with the effort of it.

We stayed there for what felt like ages, me rocking us both back and forth, still softly whispering, 'It's okay, Mummy's got you, it's okay.'

When his sobs had subsided, I felt able to ask, 'What's going on, baby boy? Tell Mummy.' And then . . . the little voice from under the towelling robe said . . .

'Santa told me I couldn't have more than one present. He said because I asked for loads that he would get me a pink dress instead!'

And with that the wails came again, like a little wounded animal, his whole body shook with it.

It hit me hard.

We had been to visit 'Father Christmas' earlier in the day. I had gone with a couple we knew well, and our four children had gone in to see Santa together. When Santa had asked Wilbur what he wanted, my boy (the youngest) had excitedly said, 'Loads of pre-sents,' smiling broadly as he did – holding his arms out as wide as he could, to mimic the amount of gifts he was imagining.

Santa replied, 'Well, young man, if you're going to be greedy, then I shall get you a girl's pink dress instead.'

I'd actually heard Santa say that and instantly thought it was an odd comment. I had felt bad for Wilbur who was just excited and, to be honest, I hadn't liked it. But I was with four kids and two other parents and, I admit, I felt unsure about speaking up and complaining. So, I didn't. And to be really honest with you, I regret that, because, as we have already seen, what might seem odd or relatively trivial to adults can be devastating to our children. If you ever get that sense with your child, NEVER be afraid to speak up if it means you protecting and helping them handle upset.

Back to the bathroom. Firstly, I engaged **STOP SN-O-T**.

- **STOP** – engage my wise owl brain – let's look at the bigger picture here . . . and see it through the child's eyes.

- It's **SN-O-T** about me – I must not take this personally – it's about something else.
- **OBSERVE** – this must be about something else? If so, what?
- **TURN IT AROUND** – let me put myself in Wilbur's shoes.

How might it feel for a little boy, not yet five, to be told off by not just anyone . . . but by SANTA CLAUS.

It must have felt unbearable.

Wilbur had felt *humiliated* and shamed by none other than Santa, and he had been sitting with that and holding it in ALL day.

Shame, as we have seen, is one of the most damaging feelings for a child to experience. Children do not find it easy to share that emotion with anyone, and, to be fair, do you readily share something you feel 'ashamed' of? And shame is unquestionably what Wilbur had been made to feel by the one and only Santa Claus. The problem is that feelings are impossible to keep stuffed down and locked away. For an under-five-year-old they will get triggered by something and they will spill out – in this case all over that bathroom floor.

I couldn't be sure what the actual trigger in the bathroom had been – the hooded robe, or perhaps Mike (another man) telling him off, just like Santa but that was less important.

When we understand the WHY we can understand the WHAT.

I admit I was shocked by the enormity of the reaction from Wilbur. Although the mean-spirited and inappropriate comment from 'Santa' had seemed odd to me at the time, I didn't necessarily think it would cause SUCH an upset. But that was because I was looking at it from my own perspective – an odd comment by an idiotic old man dressed up in a Santa suit. Idiotic and annoying – but to cause this much upset?

However, when I *really* thought about it and *considered it from the perspective of a four-year-old boy (which, in turn, made me aware of how it must have felt for Wilbur)*, I was really bloody cross.

'That smelly old Santa!' I said.

Wilbur looked up at me . . .

'How very dare he!' I laughed now in mock outrage.

Wilbur laughed too, even as his tears were still wet on his cheeks.

He looked at me again and I sensed that bond between us strengthen again as he looked at me now, I sensed longing for Mummy to make his hurt better.

I snuggled him up and continued, warming to my theme.

'That big-bellied, old boot head!' I cried. 'I am going to go back to that grotto and pull his hat off!'

And then – *the pièce de résistance* – 'I bet he smells of wee!'

At that Wilbur let out the biggest guffaw and carried on the theme . . .

Wilbur: 'Santa's a big poo-poo head!'

And so on it went ... morphing from shuddering tears to flat-out laughter in all of about ten minutes.

Now that the coast was clear, Mike put his head around the door of the bathroom, clearly relieved but also amazed.

'Wow. What was all that about?'

I said I would tell him later but that it was all okay. We were able to settle Wilbur even more with a few stories about other people who were poo-poo heads and how Mummy and Daddy had had to deal with them (let's face it, we all know a few poo-poo heads, don't we?).

When I put him to bed half an hour later, Wilbur was out like a light. The exertion of the meltdown had exhausted him. Watching him sleep, Mike whispered, 'That was extraordinary. I was in full-blown battle mode with a four-year-old. I took it so personally that he was not listening to me. I just saw him as being "naughty" and thought that if I "gave in", I would lose any discipline I had over him ... and yes, I'll admit, in that moment, I thought if I gave in then, he would grow up into a teenager who would never listen to me.'

Mike reflected if I had not been there he would have probably ended up wrestling Wilbur from the bath, slippery wet, then battling some more to get him to bed, both of them really upset and then my husband would've spent the rest of the evening hating himself for losing his temper ...

'... Kate, it took you ten minutes when it would have taken me two hours.'

 ### Man-ouevres with Mike

'I find that my own stress levels go through the roof when I see a child's actions as potentially dangerous. In this case Wilbur slipping and banging his head on the bath. I can find myself very emotional, and I know it's triggering something quite deep within my own lizard and baboon brain, as Kate would put it, because my job is primarily to protect my children, so therefore if they don't take notice of me, then I am not doing my job properly, I am weak and not a good father. This is where I have had to learn to use the STOP SN-O-T technique. If we carry on fighting, nobody wins. In fact, after a few minutes, if an onlooker listened in, it would be hard to tell who was the adult and who was the child. STOP SN-O-T really helps me in that regard. Here was me thinking it was about Wilbur being spoilt and not doing as he was told; in reality it was about an awful Santa! This is a good example of where I had immediately gone into battle because I felt it *was* a "battle", and one which I could win, but what collateral damage would my victory cost?'

THIS WAS ALL ABOUT COMMUNICATION.

When we accept the idea that **there is no such thing as "naughty"**, we can override our own baboons and not go into battle with our kids – and then something happens that actually becomes rather magical.

That is what **COMMUNICATION** with your children is capable of creating.

We build a bond with them that lasts.

It grows stronger each time we practise the art of communication. This art of actually trying to see behind the behaviour and understanding it, and asking ourselves as parents, *How can I help?*

This is not about kids 'over-reacting' – this is about us parents *seeing the world through their eyes.* What might seem trivial to us, as adults, can feel devastating to a young baboon. Remember, at this age they just don't have the experience, the knowledge or the wherewithal to reason situations out. To Wilbur, he had been shamed by Santa, and to a child of that age, that DOES feel like the worst thing in the world.

For all of us, but perhaps for young children more than most, every day will throw up little challenges and difficulties. As we know, we might not always be aware of what happened that day – our child might be too young to be able to explain it to us yet. However, if they have a meltdown that seems totally irrational, you can trust there will be a root cause somewhere.

When we can <u>understand</u> that our children's behaviour is a form of communication, and in return show them that we want to understand (even when it might not always be clear!), we do a very valuable thing indeed.

We are telling them that they can trust we will ALWAYS have their back.

Even with the almighty Santa Claus.

And that, my friends, will set you up with a relationship of love for life . . .

* * *

TOOL KIT TIP

Code Red

That experience in the bathroom led me to create a tool for both my kids to use when something happened during their day that had really upset them or hurt them and they had not been able to tell me about, either because I had not been there or not realised it had happened.

I designed this tool to enable my children to *communicate* and *express* when they'd had an event or interaction that had upset them. Something that would help when they didn't quite have the words to immediately explain it. Something like Max pushing Wilbur over at the wild nursery or Santa telling him he would give him a girl's dress.

In Chapter 6, I showed you ways to help your children release their stress physically, but here, I want to explain a tool that will help them gain some sense of release using their words.

When Wilbur dealt with that awful 'Santa' (speech marks used correctly in this instance!) he was not yet five. Expecting a child of such a young age to clearly and calmly articulate why they were upset was, let's be honest, a big ask. An unfair one, in fact. They don't have the vocabulary and, as I explained in Chapter 1, their brain is simply not capable or developed enough to do so. In turn, this might cause reticence for them to try, as they don't want to stumble over their words, and might feel self-conscious.

I needed to simplify the challenge for Wilbur ahead of the next time that something upset him. I also thought it would be useful for Clemency, too, if ever I was met with a grumpy face rather than her usual happy smile.

So, I came up with a system to enable and encourage **the essential art of communication**, a method that I still use with both my children today.

I call it **CODE RED**.

It came about when I asked my two to play a game.

'Guys if you were at school today and needed a wee but you thought you weren't going to get to the loo in time, what colour code would that be?'

Quick as a flash, they both yelled, 'Yellow!'
'What if you were really cold, what colour would that be?'
'White!'
'What about if you were hungry?'
'Purple!'
'What If you had the most AMAZING DAY – the BEST ever?!'
'GOLD!'
They were giggling and fully engaged now.
' . . . And what about if something happened that upset you?'
In unison: 'RED!'

I suggested that if things happened at school that they found hard to explain to me (or Daddy), then they could simply say they had a 'Code Red' (or indeed a yellow/white/purple, etc.). Then we could either discuss it right there or later on when we got home.

We put Code Red straight into practice. If, at the school gates, I saw that look appear on their faces, the one that told me something was up, I would just wait. Sometimes I might ask, 'How was today? Any codes to tell me about?' Before long, they would simply come out and say, 'I had a Code Red today' (or whichever colour had occurred). At first there were quite a few yellows and purples; Wilbur had more than a handful of whites and purples during his first few days at school (understandably) and these were easily resolved.

He might come out and say: 'I had a Code Yellow!'

'Oh!' I would say, smiling – no shame implied. 'And what happened?'

'Oh, it was okay, I just really needed a wee and there was someone in the loo.'

Sometimes our children are just seeking our reassurance – especially on issues that involve an element of feeling ashamed or guilty. So here I would probably say, 'Oh, okay, that sounds a bit difficult. What happened then?'

'It was okay, I found another one.'

I might sometimes follow up with an 'Is there anything a teacher could do to help you next time?'

Or if they are a bit older and in other circumstances:

'What else could you have done differently to stop that happening another time?'

This might prompt your child to feel more able to ask for help, or think more independently as they get a bit older in how to resolve some of the issues that arise during the school day.

Code Golds are always nice because, of course, you get to make sure you are celebrating the important and special stuff too! 'Mummy, I did really well with tidying today.' (HURRAH!)

Very quickly, however, the only code that was ever really referred to was **CODE RED**.

My children became freely used to saying they had a Code Red and I would then ask if they wanted to tell me about it now (on the way home from school) or later on. If you are a busy parent, this is a great way to ensure the communication between you and your child stays open and free flowing. You might create a bookmark together or a ticket that they can colour to leave you somewhere to find it or discuss when you are sitting in bed reading together at night. Or your child might want to wave it at you like a referee's red card when they leave the school gates or when you come home from work. It is a super-easy way of prompting a conversation that helps both of you to feel connected and easily resolve any outstanding problems.

If my children prefer to wait to talk to me later, it is almost inevitably the one thing they want to discuss as they climb into bed. You might find the times that your children feel more able to talk are at night-time or in the back of the car, when all eyes are not 'on them'.

So although my experience has shown me that all the colour codes are useful, it is the Code Red that helps them most when they are feeling really upset.

Clemency's Code Reds would sometimes go along these lines:

Clemency: 'Mummy, I had a Code Red today.'
Me: 'Oh, Clemency, what happened?'
'Jemima didn't invite me to her birthday party.'
Me: 'Oh, darling, that must be really upsetting?'

Belonging is one of the most fundamental elements of being

human – we are pack animals, and for our young children it is really important that they feel they belong. Remember, all these feelings will have their roots in survival; it can feel terrible for a child to feel they don't belong. Again, what might seem trivial – like not being invited to a birthday party – can actually trigger a much deeper, more atavistic reaction: a sense of being excluded from the herd. So, we must never be dismissive of how our children are feeling. Instead we might try to get beneath it and understand it from their perspective.

I pause, letting that sink in. Then follow up with: 'Do you know that happened to me just recently?'

Clemency literally sits bolt upright.

'Mummy, what happened?'

Me ... thinking furiously ... 'Well, Sarah at work invited everyone to her party and she didn't invite me.'

C: 'What did you do?'

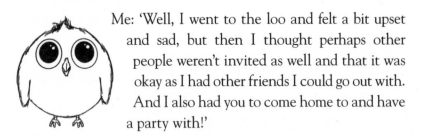 Me: 'Well, I went to the loo and felt a bit upset and sad, but then I thought perhaps other people weren't invited as well and that it was okay as I had other friends I could go out with. And I also had you to come home to and have a party with!'

Clemency's furrowed brow melted. She lay back in the bed, clearly pondering the conversation and then asked me to tell her more stories of when that had happened to me. I felt her body relax and within minutes my daughter was sound asleep. She could rest assured there was nothing wrong with her and that she could always come to me with her worries or fears, because she would always have a tribe of her own.

THAT IS THE POWER OF COMMUNICATION.

* * *

What having a 'Code Red' system does is create a form of communication between you and your child for when they can't quite find the right words to explain how they feel. Saying they had a 'Code Red', or even just holding up a red card at the end of the day, will tell you all you need to know.

It allows you to then ask a few open questions to enable you to be there for your child when they perhaps need you the most . . . without them feeling forced into asking for help (because who is good at doing that, right?).

Each time I hear my children, empathise with them (no matter how small an incident might seem) and allow them to feel they can share these things with me, it's connecting neural pathways in their brain, or what I like to think of as joining up the dots.

What you are doing when you use Code Red is actually helping to shape their brain.

That's what being a parent is about.

Wise Owl Wisdoms

∨ ∨ Behaviour IS communication.

∨ ∨ Our children might not always have the words to say how
they feel. Using **Code Red** can give them a way to do that.

∨ ∨ Rest assured: they will find their own time to tell you.

CHAPTER 8

Contracts, Boundaries and Consequences

'When you know better, you do better.'

MAYA ANGELOU, American poet,
memoirist and civil rights activist

'When Wilbur is "naughty" does he get sent to his room?'

The question came from a little girl, aged four.

'No, sweetheart, he doesn't.'

'What happens, then?'

It's a good question.

When our young baboons are just starting out, with brains that are still growing, doing and experiencing things for the first time, they will inevitably make mistakes. Our job as parents is to help model the behaviour we want to see, to show them what is and is not acceptable.

We can do that when we *help* them in their journey, not *punish* them in the process.

Sending a child to their room sends them two clear messages:

1. I cannot/will not help you with your upset.
2. Being alone is a punishment.

Leaving a child alone in a room with their 'too big' feelings doesn't help them to regulate their emotions. They are likely to either rant, rage and rebel (more likely to lead to so-called 'naughty' behaviour later) or they will sit quietly, swallowing and suppressing those all-important emotions. When our emotions and our 'big feelings' are repressed they 'sit' inside the body, literally living there. We remember the stress response that occurs when we experience emotions like anger, fear or loss. If we repress and stuff those 'big' feelings down, we don't give ourselves the chance to 'exorcise' the stress hormones that have arisen, leaving them 'sitting' in the body. Dr Gabor Maté asserts that emotions repressed when we are young lead to ailments and depression when we are older. He told me, 'Think of it this way, when we "depress" something, we are pushing it down, like the clutch on a car. Pushing down is to depress ... this is what we become if we do not pay attention to how we feel.'

With unresolved negative experiences, too, remember we will see them all stuffed in the baboon's memory sack, I imagine them like boulders that he has to carry around, ultimately in danger of dragging him down later in life. As psychiatrist and psychologist John Bowlby said back in 1951, 'Children are not slates from which the past can be rubbed by a duster or sponge, but human beings who carry their previous experiences with them and whose behaviour in the present is profoundly affected by what has gone before.'

> **Brain Box**
>
> 'When we send our children to their room, they become adults who associate being alone as a "bad thing", which is why we see adults in modern life unable to sit with themselves in the "alone". They will use TV, video games, food, alcohol, cigarettes, anything, to not feel [that] sensation again.'
>
> Psychotherapist Liza Elle

It is the same for the 'Naughty Step'.

Instead of banishing our child to the 'Naughty Step', let's banish the 'Naughty Step'.

'Naughty steps' and banishing kids to their bedrooms evokes feelings of shame, which, as we have seen earlier, we never want to do.

Humans respond to encouragement, to being supported to do the right thing, to feel empowered and WANT to be part of the pack. That baboon wants to belong, to be part of the tribe . . . so banishing our children, punishing them for mistakes they make or behaviour that they do not at this point in time have much control over, merely breeds resentment and fear, and fractures our relationship.

Let me be VERY CLEAR here – I am not advocating a lawless,

excessively liberal form of permissive parenting either. Far from it. We don't want to be overly permissive parents. Permissive parenting simply allows our child/baboons to run amok – think kids unleashed in a restaurant. Permissive parenting is not just a negative experience for adults, it is unnerving for a child, too, because they literally don't know where the limits are. Psychotherapist Liza Elle explained to me that children might feel like they could 'fall off the edge of the world' because they don't know where the limits are. But they won't figure out where these limits are by being left alone on the 'Naughty Step' or upset on their own in their bedroom.

In my opinion, neither punitive parenting nor permissive parenting work.

So, if we are not going to punish or shame our children into 'being better human beings', nor are we going to let them run amok with no guidance whatsoever, what are we to do?

It is our job to motivate our children and to bring them on board with us, and we can only do that as a team!

TOOL KIT TIPS

Contracts, boundaries and natural consequences

We have three tools in our armoury here that will help you do this, ideas that will transform your parenting experience and, in doing so, your child's life and your own:

1.   Contracts
2.   Boundaries
3.   Natural consequences

Used individually and in combination, these tools will help our children to understand what is and is not acceptable behaviour.

1 Family contract

When working with children in counselling, we will begin our therapy journey by drawing up a mutual contract. On our first session, we will each get to put things on the contract, deciding together what is important to us both. For example:

- Time-keeping
- No hitting
- Keeping each other safe in the room
- Tidying up after we have played

The list can be as long or as short as the child wishes it to be.

A contract sets out a 'boundary' around the relationship so that if either of us crosses that line, perhaps me being late one day or the child not wanting to tidy up, we can then refer back to the contract and remind ourselves of what was initially agreed. It helps keep people safe, both with their feelings as well as physically.

In a family setting, contracts can also have real value and help us, too. It is a lovely, creative and fun way for a family to communicate to each other what is most important to them.

When a family has a contract, which everyone signs up to, it can make parenting a whole lot easier because there are no blurred lines. Acceptable behaviour is defined clearly and, best of all, everyone has had a say in contributing, which means your children (and you!) are more likely to comply with what has been agreed.

All you need is:

- A large roll of paper
- Crayons, pens and paint
- Glitter, glue, buttons
- Any other fun items that your child might like to include in making the contract!

You can call it whatever you decide: an agreement, a contract, whatever you like. The important thing is that you and your children (and your partner if you have one) are all in it TOGETHER.

Contracts are not only a great way to see what is going on for your children but also in your relationship. You can check in each week to see if anyone wants to add to the contract or simply chat about any issues that were highlighted in the week.

We first established our family contract when the children were old enough to understand it. (If you have a baby or toddler, as well as an older child, you can still make a contract and 'represent' the baby by speaking in his or her voice!)

Mike and I sat down with Wilbur and Clemency and said we wanted to ask each other what was important to us all as a family, in other words, what behaviour did we want to see and what did we not want to see? We kept the language age-appropriate: 'Okay, we are going to do something fun together as a family. We all get to take turns and say what we really like to do and how we want to do it in the family.'

We each took turns to say what was important to us.

For Mike, it was time-keeping (you can take the man out of the military . . .). He explained to the children that he didn't want to 'go baboon' on them because they were late for pre-school, he wanted to walk like the wise owl and chat and have fun games on the way. The kids agreed with glee, because they knew how much more fun it was to walk with Fun Daddy rather than Grumpy Daddy! Mike drew a clock on the paper and the kids coloured in the hands and wrote beneath it 'School 09.00!'

My main issue was around tidying up and not putting sticky hands on the walls, so I stuck some buttons on the paper to represent that.

For Clemency, it was that Wilbur couldn't keep coming into her room and messing it up. She drew a big scribble with a cross through it to illustrate the point.

For Wilbur, it involved, unsurprisingly, *Star Wars*. He wanted more 'battles' with me in the mornings before pre-school, which told me he was needing a bit more 'Mummy time', so I was very happy to comply! It was also a really lovely, fun experience as a family.

We stuck the contract up on the fridge for a few months, which was a great visual reminder, but also made it super-easy for us to be able to refer to it, but before long, all the above became second nature.

It might take time, you might want to keep it in a drawer – whatever works for you and your family. You can amend and add to the contract as you wish; just make it fun and make it collaborative. This is not about you imposing your rules on the kids – this is a FAMILY agreement.

Making a family contract is a lovely family activity to do together, but it's also a great tool so that if things do get a bit wild behaviour-wise, instead of unleashing your inner baboon, throwing down the (tea) towel and shouting up the stairs to 'STOP SHOUTING!', you can use your wise owl to walk up calmly and remind them what has been agreed.

Having everyone agree to a contract and then pinning it up somewhere as a visual reminder becomes something very important and bonds the family unit. And, of course, you can include extended family members, such as grandparents, aunties and uncles, or indeed any other carers of your children, so that everyone involved in supporting your family is on the same page.

One final word on contracts: tribal communities have lived this way for thousands of years. Of course, not with a piece of paper and some glitter, but certainly a tacit understanding within the community about what is acceptable – in other words a verbal code of conduct. We can keep our contract with our own families age-appropriate, but it's a wonderful concept to have as your children grow too.

2 Boundaries

Boundaries are key in parenting to demonstrate there is a limit to what is and is not appropriate behaviour – and what we will or will not accept within the family environment. In the same way, society operates well when we abide by certain codes of conduct, we have a moral code, as it were. So, we can help our children understand what we expect from them and model that behaviour ourselves, but also lay boundaries and firm limits on what we will and will not accept in our family unit.

Boundaries are like an invisible force field that you throw up around you and your family that allows for fun behaviour but equally that there are limits.

Oooh ... it's all a bit Yoda?!

Well, yes, 'sort of ... it is'.

But these are the same boundaries that help our children have respect for us and a clear idea of what is and is not acceptable behaviour. That respect has to be two-way.

The earlier we can work together as a family to create boundaries, the better the behaviour we can expect from our children. Your children WANT to behave and please you, because they know it is better, safer and so much more fun to be IN the tribe than outside of it!

Having your family draw up a list of the collective needs that are important to them will also strengthen the bond between you all. That idea will provide the glue that holds your little community together. Your children might want more time with you to play or more time spent at the park, your partner might use it as an opportunity to let you know about something that has been bothering them, perhaps that you are always late home or they want more time together, too. Again, it's about opening up a safe line of communication, which is always a good thing.

3 Natural consequences

In essence, it is important that we show our children that actions have consequences.

For example:

If I hit my brother, he might get hurt.

If I push him when he is near the stairs, he might have to go to hospital.

If I leave my toys around, someone might trip up.

It is all part of building up that wise owl brain that encourages our children to THINK about the consequences of their actions. At this age, we cannot expect our very young ones to really fully appreciate this as a concept, but you can start to lay the foundations with little boundaries that ring-fence the potential natural consequences of their actions.

For example, on the way home from school, we might have a conversation around:

'Okay, so let's walk through what is going to happen when we get home. Wilbur, what's first?!'
'We take our shoes off and put them away!'
'Brilliant! Clemency ... next?'
'We put our school bags away and get ready for bath time!'
'Marvellous. And if we do that, what do we get more of?'
Both: 'Mummy time!'

We can teach this to our children in an age-appropriate way. Think about this not as a punishment but that in life there are consequences to our behaviour. It encourages that wise owl thinking and, again, with all the other foundations in place you are more likely to have children who work with you rather than against you if they consider the consequences of their actions.

* * *

When contracts get broken

Clearly nothing in family life is perfect, so I'm not saying it will all be rosy in the garden overnight. So, what do you do if your child or children are not keeping to their end of the deal?

It is hella frustrating when our children don't listen to us! I know, because it can certainly still happen in our household, too! So what do I do when my child/children won't listen when I ask them to . . .

Clean their teeth
Tidy up
Stop running around?

Firstly, take a step back and look at the issue from their perspective: young baboons find us parents a mere distraction when they are focused on having FUN! When that baboon is on override, no amount of contracts, boundaries or brilliant parenting might get them on side quickly and take them away from what must be 'the most excitingest thing ever!'

In these moments, we need to find a way to CONNECT so they can really SEE us and HEAR us when their baboon is on the rampage and it is jolly hard to make them stop. Let me introduce you to the next tool:

TOOL KIT TIP

Win–Wins

Let's walk through a fairly typical scenario:

It's 5.30pm, teatime is over and there is that witching hour between then and bedtime. I usually bath my kids after supper and then we are on slow time until we snuggle up for a story and bedtime.

That's the ideal scenario.

But life is often not ideal.

So, it can run like this . . .

I am frazzled, the kids are not.

In fact, they seem to have a burst of energy around this time, especially my son. It results in them running around the house, one baboon chasing the other, with me first asking them to stop and then yelling, 'STOP RUNNING!' and then feeling bad because they were only having fun. I hate yelling, because I realise I look like a big angry baboon myself.

So, I stop, take a breath, then I get down to their level and calmly explain with a smile so that they know I am not mad at them.

'Guys, come, look at me!' I say in as sing-song a way as I can muster.

In getting your child to look at you, they have to stop what they are doing and really SEE you.

I kneel, face them and ask them to look me in the eye while I explain.

Now we are connected!

Suddenly, I am not a disembodied, screechy loud voice calling out from below, but Mummy, who is usually quite fun and understanding!

'Okay, I can SEE how much fun you are having! But [natural consequence] Mummy gets scared if you are running by the stairs, as you might fall and hurt yourself. So, I tell you what, why don't we do a deal?'

This will sound intriguing to their baboon, and with any luck their wise owl will also start to listen in.

'Let's have five minutes of fun before we go to the bath?'

Past experience tells them a deal is being made and, if they disagree, they might not get anything . . . so they agree. They might not recognise it yet, but this is the WIN–WIN.

'Shall we – go outside and shout as loud as we can? Or run around the park ten times, or see who can do 20 star jumps?' (Pretty much any activity you know they love and will find exciting to do just before bedtime will do at this point.)

This is not to get them all over-excited and energised – there has to be a time limit. I have in the past used a cheap egg timer to tell us the time, but just make sure you have that in mind. Be really clear this is not about going out for a long play on the swings; this is about five minutes of play before bed, so if a park is too far away, then stick to 20 star jumps in the garden or a walk around the block. In this instance, we might go outside and have a run around or shout BUT it will be for five minutes before we then come inside for a bath and brush our teeth.

Essentially, find something that will allow your children to let off steam, connect with you in the process and establish a verbal contract that allows you to relax, knowing you have an agreement to come inside when you ask.

And, who knows, you might find it fun yourself to go out and have a five-minute run around or shout (remember that stress response) it's as good for us as much as it is for our children!

My kids usually love that Mummy has played with them and are then willing to come up to the bath, as they know there will be more playtime in the bath that follows.

It is good for me, too, as it is a way to connect with the kids after I have run around making supper, etc. and it forces me to disconnect from all the other stuff I have going on in my head.

So that's the way it SHOULD work.

What happens when your little one breaks the contract and wants to keep going after the five minutes?!

Then we have the right to get down again to their level and calmly repeat that there is a boundary.

'Okay, take a look at the time – we have had our five minutes and you agreed we would then take a bath.'

An extra tip might be to throw in for good measure, 'Shall we race to see who gets there first?' A bit of fun competition can often work wonders!

This is another way of tricking that little baboon into being competitive and quickly bypass that sense of fun it has been so immersed in.

If fun or some humour does not work, then you have to be firm. Do not shout. Do not tower over them. Just firmly and calmly say:

'We have an agreement, and if you cannot do that, then we can no longer have the games and fun before bath time.'

Remember, what we are teaching here are boundaries and natural consequences – and also that there can be negotiations and win–wins all round IF everyone listens. Once children agree to a WIN–WIN deal, it is harder for them to break it.

* * *

My final tool for when your child isn't playing by the rules that you all agreed to, or for when they've become overwhelmed:

TOOL KIT TIP

The Soothing Stair

Here is a tool for those days when you are at your wits' end and the children are just not playing ball. You've tried all of the above but it just isn't working . . .

Sound familiar?

Deploy the Soothing Stair.

Not the 'Naughty Step'. (Put that in the bin where it belongs.)

Unlike the 'Naughty Step', the difference with the Soothing Stair is that if your child is just overwhelmed and will not do as you are asking them to, you SIT WITH THEM.

I stress: you MUST STAY with your child in this moment. Don't drag them to the step, you can ask if they want to take some time with you, sitting side by side. Hold them close or, if you sense they are on overload, just say you will sit with them and allow yourselves both to calm down.

In these moments don't worry about any form of script, just tap into that wise owl brain of yours and say soothingly,

'It's okay,' repeating it over and over.

'Mummy/Daddy understands' (even if at this stage you don't).

'Mummy/Daddy can help you' (even if at this stage you are not sure how).

And 'It's okay, let it all out.'

Rocking backwards and forwards, saying the same thing over and over, remember, can be soothing for your child's brain – the lizard in particular. As Dr Perry explained earlier, there is science in the healing power of it, so trust that in this moment you are not

His words tumbled out before he had even had a chance to think, 'I felt ashamed.'

When we use force on our children, we not only stand to hurt them physically, but we hurt their feelings, too. By that I mean we can create those pernicious feelings of shame and guilt. If we smack our children regularly, it can set up a cycle of shame that will be carried into adulthood. If you find yourself losing your temper very often, it will be worth looking at Chapter 14 where we find ways to fill up our own 'emotional cup' and become better regulated ourselves (I will also list many more resources in the back of the book). I understand we might often parent in the way we ourselves were parented, but having come this far with the book it would be wonderful to see how the insight we have shared together might allow you the capacity for change in this one regard. It can only serve you and your children well.

I interviewed infant psychologist Dr Suzanne Zeedyk on this subject, too, given she lives in Dundee, and Scotland was the first country in the UK to ban smacking. 'Our culture has for a long time believed that it is acceptable to hit children. We see that as a way of managing their behaviour, and we think that they learn from the temporary pain that comes with a smack. But science has discovered that children learn about something deeper than just limits. They learn about trust. What they learn is that the people they love aren't trustworthy. They learn that those people will hurt them. They learn that those people are not emotionally reliable. This makes the world feel like a scarier place, and this changes a child's biology, because they carry more stress.' These insights can be hard for parents to think about, and it often takes courage, especially when ideas conflict with what we have been taught is normal by our culture. The most valuable thing a parent can give a child is the knowledge that they are emotionally reliable, even in the midst of tough times.

We forget this too often – our children *want* to please us, they *want* to do things together and rarely do they *want* to go into battle. When we understand stress and how it compels our young children to 'act out', we can reassure ourselves that **there's no such thing as 'naughty'**, which means we can see their behaviour as not personal. Why would a small baboon choose to go up against a raging adult one?

Wise Owl Wisdoms

ᴠ ᴠ Our children need to understand where the limits are.

ᴠ ᴠ Being creative when making contracts can help establish family rules.

ᴠ ᴠ When children understand there are consequences to their actions, it builds up their wise owl.

ᴠ ᴠ Soothing Stairs and finding Win–Wins will help with behaviour more than any form of punishment can.

ᴠ ᴠ By working *with* our children and their feelings, we build that all-important wise owl brain so in future our children learn how to manage their feelings themselves – AND to negotiate what they want without tears.

ᴠ ᴠ With gentle boundaries and working collaboratively, we become a team. Our children feel seen and heard and their needs are met, but also they understand that when Mummy or Daddy say something important, it is time to put those listening ears on . . .

When that happens, you have yourself a total family triumph!

CHAPTER 9

Why Labels are 'Naughty'

*'It is easier to build strong children
than to repair broken men.'*

FREDERICK DOUGLASS,
American social reformer

Communication and 'good behaviour' is a two-way street. We cannot expect our children to WANT to work with us and do as we ask if we are constantly undermining them or calling them names.

Calling them names . . . me?! What do you mean?!

I mean we can *sometimes* say things to our children that we would never say to our friends!

'You're crazy!'
'Don't be such a cry baby.'

'You're so difficult!'
'You're so weird.'
And, of course . . . 'You're so NAUGHTY!'

The comments that we make about, or to, our children stick. They can cause shame, embarrassment and guilt. Those feelings get right down to our core. Very often, we don't even realise we are doing it, but their baboon does and he lodges it in his memory sack, which, as we've just discussed, can quickly end up feeling pretty heavy to carry. We saw this in action with Wilbur and the smelly Santa: Wilbur had carried the weight of the shame he had felt after Santa's comments ALL day, but ultimately those feelings, that emotion and his stress response spilled out onto that bathroom floor.

We have what psychologists call a 'negativity bias', in other words a tendency to focus on negative rather than positive information. This explains why we often recall and think about insults more than compliments.

We are wise to consider this in our parenting.

Imagine how it might feel to have your partner or best friend spend the day calling you 'crazy' or 'difficult', or push back on everything you do, calling it 'a silly idea'. Consider, too, what you remember most about your own parenting – can you remember the more positive ways your parents spoke to you . . . or the more negative?

Negative labels stick, and they sting.

During my counselling training, my group took part in an exercise where we had paper labels stuck to our chests. We could not see what was written on the labels, but they included words like 'queen bee', 'joker', 'class clown', 'hypochondriac', 'bully', 'genius' and 'kind'.

My label, which I couldn't see at the time, was 'hypochondriac'. We were told we would attend a 'party' and react and engage with each person according to the description of them written on the label on their chests. When my colleagues approached me, everyone of them had the same look of concern, a slight frown on their face, with every question laboured with a 'How are you?' and 'Is everything okay?' When I said I was fine, they would follow up with 'Are you sure you are okay?'

Initially, I found it mildly irritating, that everyone was somehow judging me, assuming there was something 'wrong' with me. I felt a bit confused and annoyed. I wanted to say, 'Stop asking me if I am okay!' I found myself rebelling, playing against type, forcing myself to be more cheerful and upbeat, the volume of my voice increasing as I defiantly said, 'I'm FINE!' I then tried to turn the conversation around, but they seemed to be resolute in how they saw me.

I hated being 'labelled'!

However, after just five minutes, I found myself somewhat resigned to the situation, thinking: *What's the point of keeping pushing back?* I went along with the concern and became ever more outrageous with my replies, 'Oh, I am just SO low!' almost said with glee, as I could see it fitted with their view of me. I literally played to type. All in the space of ten minutes.

I found myself treating other colleagues differently too. One of them had 'bully' written on her label, and during the course of the 'party' she became more and more isolated. We found ourselves not wanting to approach her at all! Sounds odd, perhaps, to say it now, in the light of day, but in that setting, having been told to respond to her as her label defined ... we went with type, and the poor woman said she had felt a similar feeling to me, first of confusion and wanting to rebel against the treatment we were giving her but then resignation, and sadness and resentment at being shunned by the group.

For us as counsellors in training, this experience was a very simple yet effective exercise designed for us to think about the children we would be working with and for us not to make assumptions. It was intended to have us reflect and reassess how we viewed others, to avoid using *labels* and consider the children in our care, not as others might have 'labelled' them, but just as they were.

Negative words lead to negative thoughts and negative thoughts lead to negative behaviour. Use a negative label about your child enough times and you might get a self-fulfilling prophecy ...You are also shaping your child's sense of self, as Dr Suzanne Zeedyk explains again on the subject of shame. 'One of the fascinating things that we now know from the science of child development is that children develop their sense of self from how other people treat them. If other people respond to a child's feelings affirmatively, then children develop the belief that they are worthwhile. They believe they matter because others treated them that way. That belief isn't just an idea. It actually affects the neural pathways in their brain and the stress system in their body. That's why shame "gets you in the gut". Your value and worth as a human being is in question, and we have a physiological response to that doubt. So if we don't want children to grow up with shame woven into their physiology, the very best thing we can do is acknowledge their feelings and treat them in a way that tells them they matter.'

The way we talk to, and about, our children, is HUGELY INFLUENTIAL.

Positive language

We are not patronising our children when we are sincere in praising them for their good behaviour. The more praise they get for their 'GOOD behaviour', the more likely they are to repeat it! When we explain what they get RIGHT and endorse it, they will want to impress us. Remember, we are the leader of the pack, and there is safety in that environment. It becomes a positive feedback loop and we can use it in parenting to great effect!

'Ah, that was such kind behaviour, Clemency. How wonderful it is when you share with your brother! Wow, what beautiful behaviour!'

At this point, I must EMPHASISE:

ALWAYS label the <u>BEHAVIOUR</u>, *not* the child.

We label the behaviour, for example: kind or unkind. We do not want our children to feel defined by their behaviour; we want them to have a strong sense of self. So, again, I cannot stress this enough: label the *behaviour, not* the child. Your *child* is not unkind, but their *behaviour* might be.

We could use SAS here:

- Say what you see: 'I see you have hit your brother. That is not kind behaviour.'

- Acknowledge: 'I can see this is difficult for you, right now. You are really, really CROSS!'

- Soothe: 'I understand it is difficult when your brother takes your toy, but we do not hit. That is not kind behaviour and it is not acceptable behaviour.'

Or maybe,

- 'Ava, you are such a lovely little girl, but that was <u>not</u> lovely behaviour!'

- And I would follow up with, 'You seem really angry,' then just let that sit there so she knows that it is the anger that has driven the behaviour.

Remember, underlying our children's behaviour are their emotions, and that whole-body response caused by stress. So be attuned to what might be going on underneath before you do any labelling – your children need your understanding as much as anything in these moments. If you can observe your child in these moments and be curious about what else might be going on, it will tell you far more than any label can.

Next, you can perhaps ask a question to engage their problem-solving brain to switch gear to a more positive and proactive behaviour.

'Shall we think how we might do things differently with your brother?'

Your compassion allows the baboon to stand down, as she feels more soothed, and then you follow up with getting your child to think things through – their little owlet steps in and you achieve more progress than if you had resorted to a negative label or other punitive measure.

So, *no negative labels.*

> **Brain Box**
>
> 'Parents can affect the chemistry in a child's brain to such an extent that for the most part her stream of inner thoughts will be self-encouraging rather than fraught with self-criticism.'
>
> Psychotherapist Dr Margot Sunderland, *The Science of Parenting*

Here's another thought on labels: remember to be age-appropriate with your language. A good friend of mine yelped in pain when he stood on the infamous piece of Lego – one of the most universal of all parenting occupational injuries! – and snapped at his three-year-old boy, 'Why don't you take more care of your toys?!'

What does 'care' mean?

With a puzzled look on his face, his little son replied, 'What's "care" mean, Daddy?'

Remember, our children see things differently from us because their brains are different. The little boy didn't see his room the way his dad did: that the room was untidy ... or even why that would be a problem. To the boy, his room was splendid just as it is, full of toys and fun.

So, on two levels, using the word 'care' made no sense to him.

So, be mindful to be age-appropriate with your language. Our very young children with their fluffy owlet brains won't always understand concepts or words that you take for granted.

One final word on labels and language: we might also want

to put the word 'NO!' into our old-school bin. This is an idea inspired by a conference I attended at which Dr Dan Siegel, neuropsychiatrist and author, gave me an exercise to try, and that made me realise how differently it feels in the body to be spoken to in an aggressive or negative tone.

You could try something similar. Try standing in front of the mirror and saying the word 'No!' to yourself, as though telling yourself off. 'NO!' 'NO!' 'NO!'

How does it feel in your body? (Look at your face, too – it's a good exercise to see the face your children see when you are in baboon mode!)

Now stop and say, 'YES!' to yourself instead, in a soft soothing voice. 'Yes.' 'Yes.' 'Yes.'

You will likely feel these very differently in your body.

Imagine how our children feel when we yell. And they are not even the same size as us!

It creates a sensation inside us that is not comfortable. This doesn't mean we don't have boundaries – of course we do, as we discussed in Chapter 8 – but it is worth bearing in mind that how we speak to, and about, our children will resonate with them.

If we find ourselves saying, 'No!' more often than not, we are not telling our children what we WANT them to do; instead, we just reiterate over and over again what they are getting WRONG. In turn, that can be translated by your child that THEY are somehow 'wrong'. It's difficult to get a child on side when they constantly feel THEY are always getting things wrong. Always falling short of the mark, as it were.

Rather than telling your child constantly what they are doing wrong, *focus on what they are getting right* – or else rather what behaviour you WANT to see from them instead. If they are very young and have put pen or paint on the walls, you can show them where they CAN paint and draw. Maybe create a special space where they can go to do their artwork, create a little box with all the things that they can use, and help them to understand that the walls look horrid (use humour!) if they have squiggles on them. Make big whirling gestures with your arms . . . when your child sees you not as a big baboon yelling at them but funny Mummy/Daddy who is being kind and telling them what they CAN do . . . well, then your job is almost done! Instead of shouting 'NO!' at our little people with their already rather fearful lizard and baboon, we can work on building their wise owlet by engaging her in thought processes about the paper and where she is going to keep it and what will she draw on it. Show them some plain paper and with a smile say, 'We CAN draw on this . . . we CANNOT draw on the walls.' Well, all she ever wanted to do was draw so . . .

To reiterate my point, focus on what you DO want to see behaviour-wise, not shout about what you don't.

Using humour and kindness ourselves means we can bring our children with us so much more easily. We can do that when there is mutual trust and respect, and, yes, respect starts from birth. Understand labels and how best to talk to your young children. When we speak kindly to our children, when we model the behaviour we want to see, we will see them reflecting it back in return.

Wise Owl Wisdoms

ν ν Don't label your child.

ν ν Label their behaviour.

ν ν Positive and age-appropriate language is always a plus.

When we see our children differently, we will see a different child. When we change the way we treat our children, they will change, too. If we are not constantly criticising them, we will get so much more collaboration and they will *want* to work with us.

CHAPTER 10

Ten-Minute Top-Ups and Hero Hours

'Our children don't need presents, they need our presence.'

DR GABOR MATÉ,
author and addiction expert

October 2020. I am on my way to hospital, it's 6am. Mike's taking me in for, of all things, bunion surgery (I know) and we've arranged for a friend to stay with the children for a few hours until he can come home.

In the end, however, the procedure took far longer than anticipated, and it was late afternoon before we both returned. I was still wiped out by the general anaesthetic and, having said an initial hello to our children with a hug, I went to bed to try to sleep it off. As with most modern families today, we were, as ever, juggling. My husband had to leave for work soon after bathing the children and cooking supper, so we asked a friend to come over to help me with bedtime. She told me to rest downstairs while she got the children ready. However, at 7.30 Wilbur could be heard running at full pelt along the landing, launching himself into Clemency's bedroom, flinging her pillows around her room. I flinched, feeling helpless, unable to walk and frustrated that the children would not do as they were asked. An outsider might have observed my son as being 'naughty'. I suspected my friend rather did. The analogy of a flapping sail came into my head. In sailing, if the person at the helm takes their hand off the wheel, if they let go of the rope attached to the sail, it will flap wildly and the boom will swing around dangerously, threatening to capsize the boat. I had been the one to 'take my hand off the wheel' today, as it were; it wasn't my fault, we had all been thrown into something of disarray, but it certainly wasn't Wilbur's fault, either. Poor Wilbur. His young brain is still very much about survival, and with me and Mike being away from home for so long, and then arriving with me complete with a massive bandage and weird shoe on my foot, unable to walk and clearly in pain . . . well, I imagine it might have felt more scary to him than I'd considered. Our children are, as we know, hard-wired to depend upon their parents while they are still young. The 'scary' feelings Wilbur would have pent up during the day in our absence were now coming out to 'play'. What better way than to run them off or fling pillows around?!

In a split-second, I saw my young son, not as a 'naughty' boy refusing to go to bed, but a flapping sail, disconnected and fearful that his mum was 'ill'.

'Wilbur, I need you to go to sleep now, into your room please . . . it is bedtime – where are your listening ears?! Make a wise choice please.'

However, me calling up the stairs was not enough to make a

connection to my young son's brain when his lizard and baboon had been on red alert all day. I realised using long sentences and reason was not going to cut it.

Wilbur turned and ran into Clemency's room. I heard her squeal with annoyance. Great! Now I was going to have double the trouble! I called him a second time.

'Wilbur!'

I was annoyed and embarrassed about his behaviour in front of my friend. I had been telling her about writing this book and, here I was, now with my own children refusing to go to bed! I felt vulnerable because I could not easily walk. I knew though there would be no winners if I resorted to shouting.

Wincing, I climbed the stairs. Wilbur ran into his room. When I hobbled in, he was in bed but giggling . . . I interpreted it as a little stress release. I smiled in the dark and patted the bedclothes, saying, 'Come, Mummy will lie down with you. I think you need some Mummy time. You have not seen me all day.'

 I felt the relief in his body as he relaxed back, not only was he not being told off, but he would also get the one thing I suspected he had needed all day. To feel close to me. He snuggled under my arm and I continued.

'I can see from your behaviour that it might feel a little bit hard to have Mummy with a bad foot?'

His head whipped round and faced me. 'Why do you have to have that shoe on, Mummy?'

Then another quick-fire question:

'What did they do to you?'

And

'Does it hurt?'

In that moment, I was reminded once again how our children's 'wild' behaviour is so often simply an external representation of their internal unease. In that moment, I gave gratitude for all the lessons I had learned. I could turn the tables and remind myself to see the situation from his perspective. He didn't have the perspective of an adult. He wasn't thinking when I limped through the door: *Ooh, Mummy appears to have had a bunionectomy – nothing to give me undue concern. In fact, it's rather common for tall women of her age. I conclude the prognosis is all good.*

No, Wilbur has the perspective of a little boy who has only been on the planet for barely six years. Millions of years of evolution have taught him that adults are crucial to his survival. When I hobbled through the door, bandaged and clearly incapacitated, his brain saw one half of his survival network taken out, unable to hunt and certainly going to have big problems gathering.

Remember, to our children, things can very often seem the difference between life and death. It's not about conscious thought, it goes deeper than that. We might be living in a modern world, but our children, or more specifically their brains, have ancient survival mechanisms.

I explained to Wilbur that a bone in my foot had been growing incorrectly, it had been very painful and that the doctors needed to make it better so they had cut my foot and I needed to rest and not walk very far.

As I spoke, I called out for Clemency, as even though she's older and I knew she could understand it more, I always feel it best to address both children together, so neither felt left out or worried all alone.

I heard her padding along the landing and she asked to pull up a little chair next to the bed. She had a question, too: 'What did they do? Tell us, but remember I am squeamish!' She smiled.

'What's squeamish?' asked Wilbur.

So, we had a conversation, us three, in the dark, me in a single bed with my little boy and his head on my shoulder, my daughter, growing up fast, holding my hand by the bedside. I explained I was sorry to be out of action, but I would get better soon. I asked what games we might play while I was resting.

Clemency began to sing a song and asked if I would sing it with her so she could learn the words. Wilbur then joined in. We sang in the dark, in sweet (and somewhat surprising) harmony.

I was reminded, with a smile, of our ancestral roots, of the songs that would be sung at the end of the day, when the tribe came together to bring about healing after death, illness or the high energy of the hunt, and how healing it was to come together in the dark here, too. It's why I am eternally grateful to have interviewed people like Dr Bruce Perry, Liza Elle and all the other contributors in this book – they have opened my eyes to parenting using my own intuition and atavistic wisdoms, able to understand my children and their behaviour, not through the prism of a label or an adult's eyes, but simply through my children. This one evening could have ended very differently. I was in pain, struggling and stressed. If I had seen my children as 'naughty', I would have missed that moment of much needed connection, and my children would have gone to bed in the dark, alone with their unease.

As I said earlier, it takes seconds to ask not, 'What is wrong with you?' but rather, 'What is going on for you, right now . . . and how can I help?' It takes seconds to ask, minutes to heal and then a magic takes place, paying back dividends, an investment that lasts a lifetime, allowing us to parent in peace, to parent in harmony.

* * *

Every child needs love to thrive. That love can be felt only in the connection we have with our children. That connection can come only when we spend TIME with them. When our days are so busy and full, I know just how difficult it can be to factor in quality time with our children. By 'quality' I mean time when we sit with them quietly, one to one, exchanging eye contact, laughing together freely, focused on each other and the relationship that we have.

Quality time is not the time spent rushing to put our children's shoes on, brushing their teeth or getting their dinner ready. Quality time is when we are able to sit, without phones, screens or other distractions . . . when we sit and breathe, feeling the warmth of their bodies next to ours and the smell of their hair . . . we are reminded of how incredible it is to be a parent.

Quality time with our children is something we must prioritise **above all else**.

When we don't spend quality time, we get what I mentioned just now after the 'bunion blow-out' – the 'flapping-sail syndrome'. It's when my children start running around, flailing around like that dangerously flapping sail on the sailboat, with the boom swinging this way and that, in danger of capsizing our little family boat. All because I have taken my hand off the tiller. I know when my children have not had 'enough' of me because their behaviour will switch from that of contained, calm and compassionate children to children who squabble, run riot and don't listen. All signs to me that my children need to feel more 'anchored', if we are to stay with the sailing analogy. And they will feel more anchored or grounded when they have my attention, when they feel they have enough of my love.

In counselling, we speak of ourselves as a 'container' and that our emotional and physical health comes when we feel 'full'. When we feel a lack – an emptiness inside – we are often driven to 'fill' it with other things: food, drink, online shopping, you name it, anything that makes us feel better inside, even if only temporarily.

When we are full, we can move through life without having to stop for artificial 'top ups' from 'things' or 'external validation'. For our young children, their feeling of being emotionally 'full' comes in the care we give them, it comes with our love and attention, which allows them to cope with whatever challenges life will throw their way.

I LIKE TO CALL THIS FILLING THEIR EMOTIONAL CUP.

TOOL KIT TIPS

Ten-Minute Top-Ups and Hero Hours

We can fill up our children's emotional cup by firstly committing to just TEN MINUTES a day and ONE HOUR a week for quality time with our kids.

Ten-Minute Top-Ups

Each day, find ten minutes *per child* to spend genuine, quality time with them. Ten minutes where they get what they want from you the most – your exclusive attention. I get that modern life can so easily get in the way. I speak to psychotherapists all the time who are exasperated by what they say has been 'a triumph of economics over family life'. However, we HAVE to battle for balance, because our children (and us) are the ones who end up compromised. When we are distracted by our phones or by work, when we are not fully present with our children because, yes, there are a zillion other things in life going on, this disconnect will play out in their behaviour.

When we are physically present but not available emotionally, it can feel like a painful rejection to our children. Therapists such as Dr Gabor Maté say it's perhaps one of the most emotionally damaging things we can do to our kids: being there, but not really. It comes back to those feelings of shame ... that sense that if my parents don't want to spend time with me, well then there must be something wrong with me. We have an obligation to our children and a commitment as a parent.

'Ah, but Kate ... I haven't really got the time, though ... '
Really?
600 seconds?

Ten minutes to check in and reconnect with your child before or after a long day?

Ten minutes for you to see them, hear them and be near them? Really?

You *can* find ten minutes, because this is possibly one of the most important things you will ever do for your child.

Look at your day – what could you swap that takes ten minutes?

Looking at social media? ... I know most of us certainly do that for ten minutes a day ... scrolling through, photo after photo, page after page ...

Or maybe there are ten minutes of telly that could be swapped instead?

Have a think, it will be personal to you, but the point is: if you can find that ten minutes, your bond between each other will be transformed. I say again, the reward you get as a parent later in life will be immeasurable.

Ten minutes.

600 seconds.

That's it.

Ten-Minute Top-Ups, or 'Ten-Minute Special Time – call them what you like, just know that in the magic of those ten minutes you spend with your child you are doing something fundamental for your relationship: you are filling up that little cup to the brim – full with your love, time and attention. And that will most definitely see your child through their day or help them regulate after it. In investing in your children, with regular Ten-Minute Top-Ups, you will **supercharge** everything you have done using the tools we have discussed in previous chapters.

SUPERCHARGED, I tell you! Because:

- When we are connected to our children, they are more likely to give us full eye contact to connect with us.
- When we ask them a question, they're more likely to listen.
- They'll more happily comply with requests such as 'tidy-up time'.
- They're more likely to willingly respond when you ask for help around the house.
- Their behaviour will improve because they *want* to please you, because you are the giver of the best gift of all: your presence!

Ten-Minute Top-Ups become addictive – not just for our children but for us, too – because something magical happens when I sit with my children without an agenda, without a phone or the beep of an email coming in to disturb us, and I am reminded how lucky I am to be a parent.

You wouldn't get a dog unless you felt you could find the time to walk it. And we shouldn't expect anything less for our children either. They have the same mammalian brains that are keen to explore, to keep busy, to learn and to have fun. Puppies left alone become bored, morose and destructive. What about our children?

We need to be there in these first five years in order for them to learn how to play and be stimulated safely and constructively. Why else would we have children unless we could invest our time in the relationship we want to have with them?

My kids ADORE it when we book ourselves in for Ten-Minute Top-Ups each morning, or late at night, for some extra Mummy time.

I can hear you thinking, *What exactly happens in Ten-Minute Top-Ups?*

Answer: anything your children want! Certainly, anything that is appropriate for the time of day: in the morning it might be sitting on the floor with a puzzle or a book; it might be a battle where Wilbur demonstrates his sword-fighting skills while I try 'bravely' to fend him off with a lightsabre ... (don't ask); wrestling him on his bed; it might see me crawling around on all fours playing 'puppy'; it might see us simply flat out on our backs looking up at the clouds. Later in the day you might just read a story or simply chat about the day.

You are the genie of the lamp and your child's wishes are your commands ... it's that simple. The **MAGIC** here is in our concentration on our child in these moments.

Without distraction.

Without interruption.

Just us and our children, for ten minutes each day.

 With a cup full of love from you each day, your children will be able to stay steady, even if their cup is knocked a bit during the rest of the day, whether they are at nursery or school or whether that is by a baby brother taking a favourite toy or an older sister not wanting to play with them.

Ten minutes each day to ensure your child's cup is constantly replenished. That means that stress response, the lizard and the baboon, get to head out into the day and can endure any spills until they see you again for a top-up. Fewer meltdowns, tantrums … hmmm still not sure about having more time-ins?!

You might decide to allocate the ten minutes at one particular time each day. In the main, I find the best times are either before we go to school (between 7.45 and 8.15am) or sometimes earlier if my son has woken up at 6am! Just figure out what works for your individual circumstances.

Perhaps find a good alarm noise for the special time to begin, setting it for the same time each day with a song that your child loves or that they find soothing. Don't feel you need to set an alarm, though, that is just a tip to get the routine going. I tend not to use the alarm system any more, and we are not too time specific. I simply say, 'Shall we have some special Mummy time?' and off we go!

I also try not to time the actual amount of play, as it can be distracting (and a little insulting for your child if you are constantly clock-watching!). In fact, you may find you lose yourself, too, as you play (you may well find this time sees you filling your own emotional cup as well). Use your instincts, your intuitive parenting and go with the flow. When you sense time is almost up, you can say gently, 'Okay, sweetheart, we have a few more minutes.' If and when your child's cup is full, you will find them readily accepting of this – and besides, they know they get it again tomorrow!

It's okay to set boundaries if you have a busy schedule or school to get to, BUT IT MUST BE TEN MINUTES. Just follow your child's lead, they will show you what they want you to do.

If you find your child is resistant to stopping, or if they do become upset when the ten minutes is up, it tells you that their emotional cup is really rather empty and they are finding it hard to 'let go' of you. If you sense this, then please do try, if you can, to play for as long as possible, to help with the all-important job of filling their emotional cup to the brim!

Hero Hours

Working in tandem with Ten-Minute Top-Ups are our HERO HOURS. As well as your daily 600 seconds with your child, *ideally* we would also spend A FULL HOUR WITH EACH OF THEM AT LEAST ONCE A WEEK.

This is an hour where your child gets you all to themselves! Again, they get to choose what they want to do, it might be going bowling, going for a walk, climbing trees, colouring, a game, they simply get to choose. The only boundaries around it are the obvious ones: that it's not costing you the earth and it's appropriate for your child (so, no casinos!).

In all seriousness, given how time-poor we often are as parents, and not least when we are parenting solo and with more than one child in our care, we might all lack the quality of connection we would love to have in any given week. By booking in Hero Hours with each of our children where possible, we can at least commit to some one-to-one time, which is often all we need to repair the ruptures and challenges of a busy week.

It's important here to say we must always only ever do what we can. You can perhaps rotate the time, organising play dates for your other children, or when they have a club or activity organised; you will again need to be inventive, the key is in finding time for your child to *have you all to themselves.*

They get to choose what they want to do. With my children I'm always surprised by the simple wishes: playing a card game, baking, colouring-in, you name it, this doesn't have to be costly or complicated.

One golden rule though: no SCREENS. I would hesitantly extend that to TV or movies, ideally, because if you are watching a film, you are not really *engaging* without distraction. (Watching a movie is an amazing thing to do with your child, however, and that can be a special moment for the whole family to add alongside your hero hour).

Screen time for your children – screen time for you

Our worlds have changed enormously in terms of our access to technology and what is now available to us online, even compared with what most parents would have had access to when they were young. There have been many calls for more definitive advice about what is and is not appropriate for children under five. In an interview I conducted with child psychiatrist Dr Dickon Bevington (from the Anna Freud National Centre for Children and Families) he told me that in the early years, when the brain is developing at its fastest rate, 'what we don't use, we lose'. It's something known as pruning. He used the rather charming example that because we are born with attention to *so many* tiny details, babies are actually able to distinguish between different guinea-pig faces! Clearly, given we are unlikely to meet too many guinea pigs on the street, we lose that ability pretty quickly. But babies and young children do need to be able to read human faces if they are to interact with other humans later on, and life naturally helps us to practise – when we watch our parents and others around us, their different facial expressions, a raised eyebrow in surprise, a wrinkle of the nose in disgust, a shift in posture to become more defensive, or how the whole body can shake with joy when we laugh! (or is that just me).

All of these things help our children's brains to develop with future human relationships in mind. So it begs the question: what happens if our children are NOT practising that as much as they could be?

Psychologist and child expert Dr Aric Sigman has long expressed *his* concern about screen time and the impact it has on our children's brain development. His research has identified a higher prevalence of screen-related addictive behaviours that reflect impaired reward processing (what makes us feel good) and impulse control in the brain.

In essence, when our children's brains are developing in these first five years, they may be shaped – and not for the better – if they are intensively exposed to certain screen activities. With this in mind, the obvious question to ask is, what is considered 'intensive' and what activities are we talking about?

Certainly there have been warnings, some from organisations such as the American Academy of Pediatrics, to limit TV and screen time for children under five but there are calls for more research to be done to be definitive.

I share the concern about the increase in young children's use of smartphones, electronic tablets and laptops, given the potential impact on sleep, fitness (if they are sedentary for long periods) and also their future ability to socialise and engage with others.

I also know, however, that for all of us, especially when we are at our most frazzled, TV or mobile screens can offer some respite – an 'hour' of downtime, a 'free babysitter' – when we know our children are 'safe' (and silent) and we can get on with whatever we need to be getting on with at home.

So perhaps it comes down to balance. Perhaps it comes down to taking what we now understand about our children's developing brains and feeling more informed to decide ourselves what is, and might not be, appropriate. We all instinctively 'know' when our children have had 'too much' screen time and not enough play outside or time interacting with us. I think if you have a child under five, you might simply want to consider what feels appropriate to you, now that you are armed with the knowledge about their developing brain and how crucial these early years are for their mental well-being.

Given the research I had done, my husband and I took the decision that our children should not have access to phones or screens when very young. In that regard, we decided we must also take responsibility for OUR screen time in the home, too. Remember, little baboons feel uneasy if we are physically close to them but not picking up on their cues. This is the case whether we have a baby, a toddler or a five-year-old. Consider how we feel if/when a partner or friend picks up their phone and starts scrolling in the middle of a conversation we are having with them. If it feels like a rejection to us, we might consider what that feels like when we do it to our children! We never want our children to draw the conclusion that we prefer the company of our phones to theirs.

Just as our children crave our physical hugs, they crave our physical presence, too. We cannot give them that when we are staring at our phones.

We have <u>everything</u> we need to ensure our children's future mental well-being. With our hugs, with our love and our attention, we as parents can give our children the greatest gifts we can give in life.

 We may need to work from home, we may ourselves certainly need to feel connected to our online communities, but we know – and my husband and I are certainly not immune – how addictive phones and social media can be. When we are aware of our own habits, we can more easily change them. It is never too late to do so, not for us, and certainly not for our children.

Changes you might consider may include:

- Agree with your partner or anyone caring for your child what feels right for you in terms of appropriate screen time.

- Perhaps use the Family Contract to discuss this (in age-appropriate terms) and explain to your children why you have come to that decision. Perhaps with young children, you could say the baboon and wise owl would prefer to be out running around rather than sitting watching a screen for too long.

- Decide if you want to have screens/phones in bedrooms or keep them to one room only.

- Set your own boundaries for where and how long you will use your own devices. We try (!) to switch our phones off at 19.00 now and demonstrate to the children we 'walk the walk' when it comes to not being slaves to the screen!

- If you do have to work or need to check your phone, if you can, perhaps try to do it when your children are not around.

- When we play, I put my phone in another room so I am not distracted by buzzing emails or messages. I know it makes me a more 'fun' focused mum during my Ten Minute Top-Ups and Hero Hours when I do!

So, back to our Ten-Minute Top-Ups and Hero Hours: the more you do these, the more magic they become and the sooner you will start noticing a stronger connection between the amount of time your children have had with you in any given week and their behaviour. As soon as I see my kids start to get fractious with each other (you know, those little comments and irritable nudges between them), I make a mental note that it appears they need more of *me* to ensure that they can be at peace with each other.

With ten minutes a day and 60 minutes a week, you will find that, over a matter of weeks or months, you will see a marked change in your child's behaviour – and perhaps even a change in you, too.

Wise Owl Wisdoms

ᐯ ᐯ   The more time you invest in your children, the better the behaviour.

ᐯ ᐯ   Daily **Ten-Minute Top-Ups** and a **Hero Hour** a week will help to ensure that their emotional cups are full.

ᐯ ᐯ   It is better for our children to be spending time with us, rather than flat screens.

In the next chapter, we will come to ideas and more suggestions on what to do with, and during, Ten-Minute Top-Ups and Hero Hours. For now, just recognise and think about the absolute vital importance of spending this time with your little ones. Having these regular check-ins will be the biggest and best investment you can make with your children.

It's all there for the taking in the magic and the mayhem.

CHAPTER 11

Why We Must Always Say 'Yes' to Play!

'We don't stop playing because we grow old, we grow old because we stop playing.'

GEORGE BERNARD SHAW, Irish playwright and Nobel Prize winner

We don't have to wait until our children become toddlers to play. During your child's earliest years, their brain makes one million neural connections every single second. The NSPCC says, 'Research has shown that when an infant babbles, gestures or cries and an adult responds positively with eye contact, words or a hug, neural connections are built and strengthened in the child's brain. These interactions can be as simple as playing peek-a-boo, or where the child offers the parent a word or noise, and the parent acknowledges this and "serves" a return with another noise or word.' I like to think of this as millions of little light bulbs being switched on with every interaction. The best 'toy' for our babies must surely be the human face: it's soft, squishy, it 'lights up', it squeaks, it laughs, it certainly brings joy, and our facial expressions teach our baby the emotions of joy, disgust, sadness, anger, surprise and fear – all so crucial for healthy brain development.

The NSPCC are so convinced of the power of play and spending time with your child that in 2020 they launched a campaign called, 'Look, Say, Sing, Play', aimed at raising awareness of the huge benefits of this approach. They say, 'It's not about just singing or talking *at* your baby. Brain-building happens when you and your little one are interacting with each other. It's about taking a cue from them, and reacting to what they're doing. You could think of it like a game of tennis – going back and forth between the two of you.'

> *Brain Box*
>
> 'You don't have to change your routine to have brain-building moments with your baby. Whether it's bath-time, bed-time or you're popping to the shops, there are always moments when you can look, talk, sing and play with your baby ... there's a real opportunity for them to do it more consciously and give them the best start in life.'
>
> Chris Cloke, NSPCC Head of Child Protection Awareness

(There are lots of good resources and suggestions on the NSPCC website, see Resources.)

We are never too young, and most certainly never too old to play.

But I wonder ...

When was the last time you asked your child if they wanted to play?

It's a question that probably brings most of us up short.

Tonight, after writing all day, cooking, cleaning, collecting the kids from school, 20 minutes of exercise and all that goes in between, I am now tired and starving. So, when my daughter asked to read in bed by herself tonight, I was enormously tempted to say 'Yes'! However, I paused ... prompted by the question I ask myself most days:

Have we had enough quality time together today?

I knew the answer before I had even had time to think it, so instead I said, 'Yes, you can read, of course, but it's been a busy day today and I have missed you. I did fancy some Mummy–Clemency time, would you like some or are you happy to read?'

Quick as a flash, she replied, 'Can we play?'

She is now eight.

And yes, sometimes my heart *will* sink when it is late and I am exhausted with a million other things to do.

But I always say 'yes' to play.

I know it is too vital for me not to.

Play has a key role in our children's lives for good reason. It helps with their emotional growth and general mental health. There is a very powerful, important play system deep within us all – in that baboon part of our brains.

When we play with our children – especially rough and tumble or physical play where our bodies connect – we are enhancing the development of their wise owl brain, which helps them to self-regulate their impulses to be calm and measured, to be at one when they are alone, to sit still even – all things we value as adults, and all things we can teach our children through play.

I mentioned in the previous chapter how damaging it is to be physically present but emotionally absent with your child. One way to mitigate this is through play.

A child senses the hypocrisy of a parent who says they care but doesn't care enough to spend time with them.

I get it – as I addressed earlier, in our modern world, there often seem to be too few hours in the day, and working parents are hit from all sides. One school mum I know told me, 'I am just so tired of feeling the guilt all the time. I have three kids, a husband who travels abroad much of the time and I am working full-time. I HATE having to send my children away when they want to play, but I just don't have the capacity to do it all. I keep questioning if I am really a good mum, if I am honest I think I am a crap mum. I am stressed, drinking too much and shouting too much.'

I hear that so much. I feel it so much. So, what can we do about it?

This one is really simple: PLAY.

And I know the resistance, the tiredness, the wanting to watch something on Netflix rather than sit and play 'shops'. But when we can get past that initial resistance it really is a healing opportunity – for you, not just for your child. As I am about to explain, we don't actually have to do too much, it is just about being there with and for our children. There is something very meditative that takes place as we attune to them, watching the way their tongue sticks out in concentration or the way their brow furrows, and the warmth of them as they lean into you but are still completely absorbed in their play.

That one Hero Hour a week and Ten-Minute Top-Ups each day – one-on-one with your child – will go a very long way towards refuelling the parent–child relationship that might have been running on empty due to our often conflicted modern lives.

So, my next tool is the simplest in this book, but also quite possibly one of the most powerful.

TOOL KIT TIP

Ask your child if they would like to play

I promise you that taking the initiative and asking your child to play will be one of the most life-affirming, rewarding and beneficial decisions you will ever take as a parent.

So, the next question is likely to be: 'What do you mean by "play"?'

First and foremost, the answer to that is, 'Whatever your child wants.' This is the most wonderful opportunity for your child to be in charge, to take the lead, to have some of the control our children crave in a world where increasingly they get so little.

There are obviously a few boundaries you need to observe: no super-high adrenaline games five minutes before you expect them to fall asleep; maybe not piggy-back racing up a hill with Grandma. All jokes aside, play does not mean we can throw paint at the walls; play does not mean we can hit each other when rolling around on the floor; play does not mean the mess does not get cleaned up afterwards. If you want to be sure these boundaries are adhered to, then a Play Contract can be really useful (as per the family contract in Chapter 8).

 Within reason, however, your child decides what you are going to play (it fuels that baboon need for some independence as well as giving them a little more control over their lives); for example, last night, Clemency asked to make a fairy garden with some small figures, mushrooms, fairy figures and hedgehogs. Wilbur often asks to play with his lightsabres or Lego.

The choice is theirs.

Now, here's a quick warning: you might already have scheduled in Ten-Minute Top-Ups or even a Hero Hour, or this might be the first time you have broached it, but when you ask your kids if they want to play, they might say 'no', in which case there is a question for you to answer: why not? Perhaps they are mad at you for being at work all day and want to 'punish' you. Perhaps it's the first time you have ever asked that question and they are so shocked they are not quite sure what you mean by it! And, always, read your child: were they engaged in something else at the moment you asked? If so, let the idea process for a bit until they are ready.

There may be many reasons, but don't worry.

Once you have asked, leave it. They will have received the message that you are open for playtime, and they will come back to you, believe me. Stick with it – at heart every child wants to play with their parent, so watch out for that million-watt smile as they gleefully shout 'Yes!'

If (when) they say 'YES', then bingo!

Getting back to what exactly 'play' is, well, I'm not sure about you, but I don't recall my own parents being particularly playful. I'm not sure it was a 'generation of play' and certainly our hard-working parents did not necessarily feel they had much time for it. So, don't give yourself a hard time if 'play' feels alien to begin with. The key here is in the connection with you. I'm not asking you to sit for hours, very often, once your child is settled in their play, the magic touchpaper is lit and the play takes over, and they only need you for a short period.

I realised that if I invested my energy at the start of play, when my daughter was telling me what she wanted me to do – perhaps being a 'puppy' or speaking as a 'doll' – that rather quickly afterwards she then took over and began to take on those things herself. My son is the same, and I have reflected it might sometimes be that we need to help our little ones to start the play, and then, when they are fully absorbed and don't need us as much, it allows us to back off a little and either sit and observe (which is frankly more magical than stacking the dishwasher), or do other little jobs, either in the same room or in my own ... gradually moving downstairs when or if we need to. I have lost count of the times when my children have asked me to play and in my head I think of all the things I REALLY NEED to get done, but when they ask for 'Mummy time', the answer will always be 'yes'. Inevitably, it really is for a short period, as my children get their 'fix' of our play and we can then move on, either to reading a book together or I can nip to my bedroom to 'tidy up' or downstairs to do some work or start dinner while they carry on quite happily. So please, *please* know it will be worth the time that you invest now for the massive reward that plays out in your relationship later!

If you have never been taught to play, then you might feel uncomfortable to begin with or even maybe at a loss as to essentially HOW and WHAT you can play. It's a constant refrain, and I know my husband would concur with this. He preferred to take our children to the park, to climb trees or paddle in the stream in our park, because that is what his father had done with him. But often our children would also ask, 'Daddy, can you sit with us?' And Mike initially found that hard. Until I explained, 'You don't need to play in a baby voice, you don't need to play at being a monster if you don't want to, you just need to be present, to show an interest, to show up.'

All adults can play. Find what you are comfortable with, but equally when you follow your child's lead, you might be surprised to find you can enter any world they invite you into. Just sitting and being with them makes for a great start.

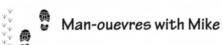 **Man-ouevres with Mike**

'I think dads (especially ones like me who did not have playful parents themselves) do find it difficult to play. I thought it was just me and that I might be a bit crap, especially when Kate's so brilliant at it – and I didn't really know how. Like she said, I knew how to take the children to the park and do pull-ups on trees or go running or play football – all great things to do, as my children love being outside – but sitting down and playing was not something I felt I could (or wanted) to do. One day I sat down with Wilbur and just asked him, "Do you want to play?" and his gratitude made my heart melt. I then had to resist the urge to organise and suggest things – rather just sit back and go with the flow. The children are great guides: they literally tell me what to do! Kate's right – it's actually really relaxing when you can just sit there with them, not worrying about whether you are doing it right. If we let them take the lead, they will soon show us, and it's so calming simply to watch them as they play, too.'

Okay so if you are not already a play Jedi Master, here's a few tips on how to get the smoothest, easiest pathway to the Great Galaxy of Play!

- Keep your voice light and fun.
- SMILE!
- Be prepared to let your child take the lead ...

Given we adults control most other aspects of our children's lives, it can be incredibly annoying when we also try to determine how and where our children PLAY, too: 'Oh, not the sand, it's too messy!' Or, 'Argh, not the paint. No, no, let's do it here, shall we play with the cars instead' ... and so on.

If you see or hear yourself doing this, try to STOP and reframe:

- When we play with our kids, we must allow THEM to be in charge.
- When we play with our kids, it is EASIER than we think.
- Play can be enormously therapeutic for both us and our children.
- We just need to be with them, watch what they are doing and, very occasionally, 'reflect' or say out loud what we see.

You want children who can fully embrace play with you, unafraid that you might yelp or snap at them for some reason they can't possibly yet even understand. Play is genetically ingrained in us all, but it needs the right environment: your child has to feel psychologically safe with you to be able to 'let go'.

Set up your play time to succeed – rather than arranging it at a moment when it is more likely to fail. For example, if you have a busy schedule and know you have work to do, find time on a day when you know you won't both be tired. If you have more than one child, it would be great if another adult could give the other child attention so they are separated. Nothing spoils special-time play than having siblings fighting over their parent's attention!

Just ten minutes can be magical, remember?

So here we go . . .

Let me give you an example of the sort of play that my kids love. Get some bubble mixture, some crayons, sheets of paper, some sand in a tray, maybe some plastic animal toys, some finger paints (big tubs are great because we can put our hands in – yup, it's going to be messy!), a large plastic sheet or wipe-clean tablecloth. If you can go outside, so much the better, then you really can let loose . . . because we do need to let loose.

There is a very good chance that your child will just dive straight in and begin playing, as they will be so excited with your presence. If they are more reticent, just gently make some suggestions, but don't try to direct too much. Just show them the paint tubs, the paper, crayons, the animals and the sand tray . . . run your hand across the sand even and ponder out loud in a soft voice.

'Hmm, I wonder what we can do together? We have the sand, we have the crayons . . . '

Don't overload or overwhelm your child. Allow them to consider. Then follow up with . . .

'Wilbur is in charge, so you get to tell Mummy what you want to do MOST!'

And you will be off and running.

Once their baboon (their play system) is activated, it will compel them to take charge and tell you exactly what it is they want.

Now all you have to do is LISTEN. Keep questions to a bare minimum, as it can interrupt your child's thought processes.

Just sit still and notice what they are doing. And simply reflect on it. That's it.

That's as hard as it gets.

- 'So, you want to play Batman and Robin!'
- 'Ah, so you are going to take the doll from her cot and put her in the pram.'
- 'Ah, I see the dinosaurs are fighting.'

This is all about what you SEE.

Which, translated into your child's world, tells them **YOU SEE THEM**.

This creates a rather special environment where the child feels increasingly safe to express themselves. In turn, the play will help their developing brains start to self-regulate and to work out more complex emotions and thoughts, all in a safe and fun way.

Play is so potent for your child's future well-being and mental resilience.

Parent ponders: Alpa, mother to a two-year-old

'Playing with my two-year-old son is such a special time. He is my first child, so, I admit, it's tricky to know how to engage him in play, and also whether to make it educational or not. Quite often, he will direct me to what he wants to do. For instance, when he is playing with his train set, he likes me to set it up and help get the train over a bridge. But then he will often want to drive the train around the track on his own; he seems quite independent like that. If I leave him, he will often ask me to come back and sit with him. I would say the most difficult part of play is sometimes finding the patience or listening to him when I'm tired. I've noticed if I try to force him into a game, he doesn't really respond positively. He often wants to do it his way, so I just let him. Whatever we are doing, I love our time together and, as he grows, it's lovely to see him developing and changing.'

Alpa explains what many of us may also have seen in our own children. Very often, our children just want us to be present, they don't *need* us necessarily to actually play, but observing them and asking gentle questions to let them see you are really engaged is often enough. It is clear in these moments how little we need to do but how much our presence makes the difference.

Alpa also asked whether she should be directing her son in any way: 'I do try to practise colours with him and numbers, but he really doesn't seem very interested.'

As I said at the very beginning of the book, for our children under five we really don't need to worry about 'educating' them during these moments, their play is educating enough. When we allow our children to 'take the lead', to direct us where they want us, and sit back when they don't, the magic really happens: we give our children an important element of autonomy whilst providing the safety of the space they need as well. That is hugely empowering. It is affirming for them, too, that you care about them enough to want to simply be there for them at these moments!

In engaging with our children, in saying yes to play, we are telling them they MATTER to us, that we WANT to spend time with them, not evoking those feelings that they are too boring to play with or not exciting enough. These are not messages we *ever* want to give our children, and so by simply investing a short amount of time at the start, we all get a win.

There is a healing power to play too. Sometimes your child's unconscious mind will guide the play. You might find your child has two figures fighting, or one might be 'bullying' the other, they might be animals, they might be people, they might be blocks. Whatever they are, your child will now be 'speaking' in metaphor; that is to say, they are telling the story through the toys.

Don't worry, you don't have to be a therapist here, you are not expected to analyse your child in these moments. What I will say is that the more you play with them, the more patterns you might be able to see playing out. Einstein said, 'Play is the highest form of research,' and he was right; it is also the best best best way of connecting to your children and for them to connect to you.

In general, avoid over-questioning – simply having you there when your child is engrossed in their play is enough. If you do wish to ask questions, try not to ask closed ones, namely those that solicit a 'yes' or 'no' response, or questions that are too specific, such as, 'Is that toy really Susan who you said bullied you today?' This risks jolting your child out of the beauty of their play.

Questions you might want to try in a soft voice, just gently to ask:

'And who's this?'

'What's happening here?'

'I am wondering what it is like for the dog/bear/car over there . . .'

If you sense something is going on for your child, perhaps you could say:

'These two are fighting a lot aren't they?'

Or

'Ah, I see the elephant has just pushed the lion over.'

Your child might or might not go on to explain that the elephant is a nasty bully and made the lion cry.

Don't push that, let them talk in their own time.

Try to ask open questions:

'What is this one doing over there?'

'What happened there?'

'What's going on here?'

'What is this one doing?'

If they want you to play a character you might ask . . .

'Okay, tell me about this one. What does their voice sound like?'

Your child might say, 'Oh, she's lovely, she has a soft voice,' or they might say alternatively, 'Oh, she's mean, she has a cross voice!'

And go with whatever your child tells you – gently. Be guided by your child in the play, so if the character you are playing is cross, you can be gruff rather than aggressive!

If one character looks a little sad, or on its own, instead of saying that explicitly, you could say something like,

'Sounds like that could be a struggle?' Perhaps ask:

'What is life like for him?'

'What does he like to do most in the world?'

'What does he like to do least in the world?'

'Tell me about that . . .'

'What is happening now?'

Your child might well act out what is going on around them; for example, if they are anxious about anything, or perhaps if you and your partner have been arguing, or if there has been a bereavement or big emotional upheaval in the household. Whatever it is, it's okay. Firstly, it is good for you to be aware that your child has picked up on that; secondly, it should reassure you that they feel safe enough with you and empowered to express any anxieties. If there are issues that you are concerned about that might be affecting your child, or you, I would always clearly stress speaking to your children's school or a charity like the ones I list in Resources at the back of the book. There are many wonderful children's mental-health charities, all of whom have excellent resources online, too, so they can prove an invaluable guide for you and your children.

So, please do not worry. Consider it this way: whatever your child does in his or her play is going to be a good thing if it means the stress (if there is any) is coming out, which is far better than anxieties remaining within.

Above all don't sweat it. You are not there to be a therapist to your child. Just sitting with them in a quiet ten minutes of play is enough for them to feel grounded with you and build on that all-important connection they feel with you. There is much evidence to show that healing can take place even in these shortest of periods, when you are really present for your child, there is truly a magic that happens in our play.

Remember, too, that relationships are key to helping our children's stress response. Our children are more resilient than we think when they have us by their side.

Here are a few more tips on play, inspired by my training to become a counsellor with Place2Be (see Resources):

Preparing to play

Sit comfortably – probably on the floor – and mirror your child's body language if you can, so that if they are sitting cross-legged, you do, too.

Mirror their tone If they sound excited, so can you; if they speak in hushed tones, so do you. The more you are attuned to your child in their play, the more you observe them, the more you get to know them, then the more they sense they are really being 'seen' by you.

Use lots of reflections What I mean by that is simply reflecting back what your child is telling you; for example: just repeat the noises they make, 'Whooooosh'! 'Wheeee!' or 'Oh, so this one is really happy/cross right now?' You verbally reflect back to your child what you are seeing without judgement or comment, so you might say, 'I see you chose the horse and the car to play with.' In doing this, your child will feel connected to you, because you are seeing what they are seeing. Literally say what you see – it is no more complicated than that.

Don't think you have to make sense of anything Your child is working it all out for themselves – or, rather, their unconscious is.

Avoid asking 'why' questions, as it means your child has to move away from feeling and has to start thinking. This stops their flow and, frankly, sometimes they just might not know.

Stay in the metaphor By that I mean your child will often tell stories through their play, but the story might not seem obvious because it is told through figures, imagery and symbolism.

Play is so simple, so beneficial, so hugely rewarding. SIMPLY BEING THERE with your children will give them the comfort of your presence and the security that you are there for them; in turn, this will allow them to relax into play in a way that is actually healing and calming for their lizard and baboon brains.

Let me give you one final example, and one of my husband's favourites: water pistol fights! One summer's day, Wilbur asked me to make 'Mummy time' a water pistol fight, and I admit that I was initially resistant. I was not really in the mood to get wet.

Despite my reluctance, I agreed, always propelled by the notion I have to SAY YES TO PLAY! and we ran outside with pumped-up water pistols (which had a surprisingly long and, dare I say it, satisfying range). We had the BEST 20 MINUTES! I squealed as Wilbur in brilliant baboon-play mode soaked me, and I returned fire. It felt good to have this water gun in my hand and I suddenly understood the appeal of why he was constantly pointing it at everything in the garden. At the same time, I also felt awful that I had always previously shouted, 'No, please don't wet the windows – they will mark. No, please don't wet the grass, it will make my newly cleaned floor all muddy when you come in ...'

Oh, for goodness sake, what a fun sponge Mummy has been!

Once we finished the water pistols play, Wilbur immediately requested that I read a car book to him. He sat between my legs and we flicked through the pages of colourful supercars and fast machines, I smelt his hair and kissed his cheeks as we went through the book, with him pointing out the different types of cars on the pages, asking me if I had 'ever been in one of those, Mummy?'. Then, like an exhausted but contented puppy, my beautiful little playmate crawled into my lap and gave me the longest hug we'd had in a very long time.

It was magical.

It is in these moments that healing truly occurs. It is in these moments that we remember why we became parents and why our children have our hearts.

Wise Owl Wisdoms

ᕏ ᕏ   There is a power in play.

ᕏ ᕏ   Follow your child's lead.

ᕏ ᕏ   Play reconnects us with our children and can help to repair any emotional ruptures that might arise through any given day.

We are social beings, we love our children and we want to be good parents. In fact, we want to be *great* parents! Modern life might compromise us but we don't have to let it compromise our children. We just have to find different ways of carving out our time with them.

And we must carve that time out.

If we are not present for our kids, they get about 10 per cent of us, if that.

And that's not enough.

So, go on . . . what are you waiting for? . . . go ahead and make their day: ask your child if they want to play!

CHAPTER 12

Siblings – How to be a Squabble Stopper

'*Siblings: children of the same parents, each of whom is perfectly normal until they get together.*'

SAM LEVENSON, humourist,
writer and the youngest
of ten children

I heard the click and turn of the key in the lock as I was cooking supper recently. The clunk as the door opened and then my husband's voice. He was home after two nights working away, but instead of shouting a cheery hello he was speaking in hushed tones. Slightly on edge, I wondered if he had brought an unexpected guest home for supper. Exhausted, having been on my own with the children, I had been looking forward to seeing him and I didn't want to have to entertain tonight.

Before I got to the hall step I heard a woman's voice. It was unfamiliar. Her coquettish laugh came in response to something he had said. My stomach lurched.

I stopped in my tracks, startled, as Mike paused then called out, 'Look who I have brought home!'

The children came flying down the stairs just as I entered the hallway. In front of us was a beautiful woman beside my husband who stood, his arm around her waist, pulling her to him as she looked adoringly at him.

With a dopey grin on his face, he turned to me and said, 'Isn't she beautiful?!'

What the actual . . . ?!

His hand dropped to hold hers and they came towards me.

'Darling, this is Dahlia, come say hello, isn't she gorgeous!'

I thought I might be sick.

Then I reasoned: *Okay, this is just a really, really stupid joke, a really, really bad one, but surely a joke?*

'What are you talking about?' My voice is low. I can't even look at her. 'What's with all the suitcases?'

'I told you I was bringing someone special home! She's come to live with us!'

The next two weeks passed in a blur and I was in shock as friends arrived to congratulate my husband (and me) on the new addition to our family. Dahlia was given beautiful gifts and everyone kept telling her how beautiful she was. I felt invisible. I ran to the kitchen and stayed there. I couldn't bear it. I hated my husband and I hated her.

And breeeatthe . . .

My goodness I hated writing that story. Just the very idea of it makes my blood run cold. (Mike says he even feels guilty reading it!) I was inspired to write that by authors Adele Faber and Elaine Mazlish who, in their parenting book *Siblings Without Rivalry*, tell an oft-repeated story, a joke, about a man who brings home a second wife. I think it helps us to consider **what it might be like for our very young children when we bring a baby brother or sister home from hospital. It can really feel like a SHOCK.**

No matter how much we might prepare them for it, NOTHING can ever compete with the realisation that this new addition means they'll now have to share the love of their parents!

We wouldn't want to have to share love in our own relationships – why would we think it easy for our children to do the same?

This scenario clearly never played out for me in reality (thank the Lord), but of course it _is_ playing out for lots of little boys and girls, currently the centre of their parents' universe and now forced to welcome a stranger in the form of a newborn baby who threatens everything they hold dear.

Now ask me why there is such a thing as sibling rivalry?!

Why do my children fight?

Sibling rivalry has its roots in evolution.

We see it in many aspects of the animal kingdom, from eagle chicks through to hyena cubs, many of whom will die in the first few months of birth having been killed by (mostly older) siblings in the competition to survive.

Our children still very much depend upon us, their parents, for survival. When a sibling arrives, there is immediately less space for them in the 'nest'. No matter how much we try to make it otherwise, our first-borns *have* to share our affection when a new baby enters the household. We are naturally compromised by having a newborn to care for and all that entails. If we consider our baboon and think of him in his troop, we might readily appreciate how being displaced can feel. To a young baboon that can feel very dangerous indeed. There is suddenly competition because, 'If Mummy loves you more than me, I might be the one to get left behind.'

In other words, *'If something bad happens who will Mummy rescue first?'*

That's the unconscious of a young child, a child with an ancient brain that has been hard-wired over hundreds of thousands of years.

The fear for our children when we bring another child home is REAL, the resentment is real and the resulting competition can be fierce.

Think back to my dreadful nightmare scenario with another woman being brought home, an immediate competitor for my husband's affections:

- Wouldn't *you* want to shove her straight back out the door?
- Might you want to slyly nudge her when you could, or ignore her?
- You're certainly not going to share anything with her or, heaven forbid, play games with her!
- Wouldn't you want to make her feel so unwelcome that she would soon want to leave?
- And if she didn't leave? Might you feel forced to compete with her in order to regain your husband's affections, or perhaps to 'act out'? Anything to get his attention.

Love is an enormously powerful emotion. It connects us and makes us feel safe. When we are loved, we feel that we belong, that we matter.

So, too, is the opposite – jealousy – or that negative, emotional pain that is *also* felt by a child as he watches his mother kiss and cuddle the new baby. The resentment can be *very* real.

We try to *prepare* our children as much as we can, talking about baby, having them pat the bump, talk to the bump, taking our children to hospital scans, even giving them presents from the baby. But given nothing can prepare any of us for the overwhelm of bringing another child into the home, we cannot surely expect our little ones to truly appreciate the concept, and certainly not the reality. Adding a new baby to the family can turn all our worlds upside down, not just our children. Not for nothing is this the subject of thousands of anxious debates on parenting sites around the world.

We cannot expect them to readily accept a newborn baby arriving in the house. Therefore, let's take a moment to fully take on board that:

1. Sibling rivalry is <u>normal</u>, it stems from the <u>evolutionary concept of 'survival of the fittest'</u>.
2. Almost all families with more than one child will experience it at some point.
3. We do well to address this if we are to create a peaceful family environment now, and in the future help our children to become firm friends for life.

So let's see how we can become super-powered SQUABBLE STOPPERS! Firstly, let's look at some of the underlying factors of WHY some children might squabble more than others.

You may have sometimes asked yourself ... why do my children fight more than others?

The age gap

Research suggests having a minimum three-year age gap between children might see less direct rivalry, as the older child will not only have enjoyed the full attention of the parent/s for three full years, but it is also at the point of development when they might actually enjoy having more independence. Therefore, they might happily take on tasks like helping change a nappy or preparing food for the new sibling, as it serves to help them become more independent as a result. Compare that with a one- or two-year-old who still needs help with going to the loo or with feeding and is just not ready to become more independent. This child can naturally resent having less of their parent/s at a time when they need them the most.

Early research by Weston A. Price – a dentist who travelled widely in the early 1900s, visiting communities around the world and looking at optimum health and nutrition – found that in many traditional cultures, there tended to be a 'natural' three-year gap between one child being born and the next. In traditional cultures, women could breastfeed for longer and the age gap allowed their bodies to repair and refuel after the rigours of childbirth and child rearing.

Modern life often means we don't have the luxury of waiting (of course, sometimes it just happens that way). I had my own children at 41 and 43, both conceived naturally and spontaneously. I certainly never had the luxury of choosing when I had them or how much time I had between them! That said, I can certainly see now how having a little bit more time between children would have been very helpful!

I'll add a sweetener in that research also suggests siblings close in age are likely to be very close when they are older, but no question, parenting siblings close in age might very well put you through your paces.

Gender

Gender might also be considered a factor in how smoothly your siblings get along. Same-sex siblings, especially boys, might be more likely to fight or compete with each other. While we are on the subject, a word about this topic and boys. Naturally, we want to parent by personality and not by gender, but it is important to note what science tells us. Psychologist and author of *Raising Boys*, Steve Biddulph, explains how: 'Boys of about four years old are often particularly energetic. Around this time, their bodies release the luteinising hormone, which stimulates special testosterone-making cells in their testes, in readiness for puberty. While the science of this is still poorly understood, parents tend to notice a surge in activity at this age.' There are studies that look at behaviour in four- to five-year-olds and have found that boys and girls do have different ways of playing and communicating.

Steve Biddulph picks up on these differences with language development and explains that at four years boys start towards their real boyhood, and for many of them that includes a great need for movement and action. As he says in his book, *Raising Boys*: 'It's a serious parental challenge to find ways for our boys (and girls) to express their physical energy safely and sociably, and still stay connected to them and their feelings, so they know they are loved. In fact, the whole challenge of being male, lifelong, is learning that it's possible to be energetic and safe, boisterous and thoughtful, adventurous and responsible.'

Parent ponders: Ali, mum to twins, aged five

'I think it helps us as parents to realise and appreciate the differences between boys and girls, and again realise that this is normal. I think that we so want our children not to be limited by gender labels that we deny the differences of energy, ways of learning, skills, etc. So my daughter will sit, draw, read and write, while my son, her twin, resists all those and wants to fight and move. Schooling is so pressurised so early, and as a parent I so want my son to do okay that it can all become too much. During lockdown and home-schooling that pressure really came out – from the school, from me and through to him. So I was forcing him to sit, shouting at him to do his work, pleading with him to try – only leading us both to tears and anger. As a mother, as a believer in positive parenting and discipline, I knew that this was wrong and counter-productive, and yet it became a daily cycle. When I spoke to Kate it brought me back to what I knew: my son wasn't ready, he was a boy, he was a baboon, he would learn in his own time later when he became inquisitive. He was NORMAL. I could breathe again!'

Siblings close in age but different genders can also struggle, especially if the boy is the younger of the two. I have personal experience. My little boy is almost as tall as his sister despite the two-year age gap and he was constantly seeking to usurp her in the 'pecking order'. We do not want to have one child constantly trying to assert control over another. It can set up an unhealthy dynamic for both, both in their sibling relationship and with other children and in adult relationships later in life.

Temperament

Temperament is another factor. One child might be an extrovert who loves playing games that are boisterous and energetic, while the sibling might prefer to sit quietly and play alone. We know ourselves that certain personality types either get on well or mix like oil and water. A good friend who is a psychotherapist of many years advised me when I became a mother for the second time that I must not try to force my children to become anything other than themselves and help them find the common ground between them as they played. For an extrovert child, this might be by helping them to *contain* their energy when they play so they learn impulse control, to better *contain* their emotions. For a more introverted child, confidence in play comes when we help them to find and use their voice. You do this by investing time in your children, giving them the space to play, encouraging them to feel the range of their feelings and having an open line of communication between them and you. This way you can bring their sense of self to its full potential and not try to change it.

The trick is to work *with* each child's character and honour them as they are.

Let's be honest here: you'll find your children will fight over toys, food, who gets to press the elevator button – you name it – but why? It's not because they are 'naughty' – because there's no such thing!

It's simply that baboon back in the driving seat again. Let's take a look.

Sibling flashpoints

1 Sharing

I've heard it said that 'Sharing is caring', but it's really not – at least not to a young child under three.

For a very young child, being forced to share can be rather stressful.

Heather Shumaker, parenting author of *It's OK Not to Share*, puts it this way: 'Traditional sharing expects young kids to give up something the instant someone else demands. Yet we don't do this ourselves. Imagine being on your cell phone when somebody suddenly comes up and asks for your phone or takes it from you. "I need to make a phone call," he says. Would you get mad? As adults, we expect people to wait their turn. We might gladly lend our phone to a friend or even a stranger, but we want them to wait until we're done. The same should apply to kids: let the child keep a toy until she's "all done." It's turn-taking. It's sharing. But the key is it's child-directed turn-taking.'

In Squabble Stopper world, a parent would help their child to decide when to share. So, rather than saying to the child with the toy, 'Five more minutes, then it's Arabella's turn,' we use our inner SQUABBLE STOPPER and help our children to use gentle boundaries but also have empathy – understanding the toy is important to their sister, too – so they might say to their sibling, 'Arabella, you can have it when I'm done.'

We'll look at this in more detail, but let's just remind ourselves WHY it can actually feel STRESSFUL for our very young children if they are forced to give up something they are enjoying or perhaps even need in that moment. As we  now know, their brains, especially under three, are driven by the evolutionary principle that having enough food or possessions could be the difference between life and death, so why would they willingly give them up?

Take the example of the everyday sibling issues that can cause such unnecessary grief, like which child gets the blue plate today or who gets the yellow ball to play with. It drove my husband insane in our house, until I asked him to look at it from the perspective of two young baboons driven by survival instinct. To these siblings, these things feel like they really matter a lot. He looked at me and said, 'Right. Simple solution: let's just buy two of the same and take the problem away!'

Keep it simple: take away the strain – go for the same.

If your young children are fighting over the small stuff – don't sweat it – SQUABBLE STOP it and just buy two of the same for each: two blue plates, two yellow balls, the same pyjamas, whatever they're arguing over. Don't sweat the small stuff.

'Controlling the surroundings', as my friend Steve Mann says in his brilliant puppy-training book, *Easy Peasy Puppy Squeezy*, is what we need to do to prevent unwanted behaviour. Well, I hate to say it, but this applies to our children, too. Sometimes with siblings it really is just about 'controlling the environment'; just as we take away our best shoes from a puppy's reach, so we can take away the thing our children are squabbling over, often resources, and remove the source of the squabble – simples!

As your children get older, around four or five, they'll *want* more independence and their own individual things. You can then give them the option of either having the same or choosing their own different-coloured items. Giving our children choices is a good thing, too. It encourages them to grow their sense of self – the feeling that they can become their own person who can make healthy choices and set their own boundaries. **The Family Contract** (see Chapter 8) can also be very useful in establishing and maintaining ground rules for this. Choices or decisions they make can be put on the contract, either as a picture or written up, so everyone can be reminded of it ahead of or during any potential future squabble. 'Clemency has the blue cup, Wilbur has the red'.

We might accept that children can become incredibly attached to toys or possessions and invest a lot emotionally in them. For any *Toy Story* fans, we saw this with four-year-old Bonnie and Forky Fork in *Toy Story 4*, where she had an absolute love of, and need for, the company of a fork she had made into a toy at pre-school. She had invested her emotional capital into that fork, given she had been nervous about going to pre-school. Toys will often hold emotional value for our young children and we are wise to recognise and honour that.

If your child is playing with a toy, and another child (a sibling or friend) asks for it, please don't feel obliged to force them to hand it over, because:

1.   It can fracture the relationship you have with your child, as they see you as the enemy because you didn't 'have their back' when they needed you to.
2.   They will perceive this as you favouring the other child, thus confirming their worst fears that you *do* love their brother/sister more than them (and make them resent their sibling even more).
3.   It implies to them that their needs don't matter as much as someone else's.

We <u>want</u> our children to become generous-spirited and kind. We want them to notice and acknowledge the needs of others and empathise with them.

What we <u>don't want</u> is for our children to think they should give up what they have simply because another child asks for it. We <u>don't want</u> children who become adults who have been conditioned to put other people's needs before their own. And that last point is important. If we force our children to give up their cherished possessions simply because someone else wants to play with them, we are implicitly telling them their needs matter less than the other child's.

So, what do we want to achieve here? We want children with:

- **Empathy** Where a child recognises and notices if another child would like a turn of their toy.
- **Impulse control** Where a child can use their words rather than snatch.
- **Team skills** A child who understands they can share in a way that everyone wins.
- **Negotiation skills** A child who can find that win–win for everyone, but not give up their own.

These skills will see your child become an empathetic, generous-spirited, self-assured adult. But *not all children under five are able to do all this by themselves* (yet).

So how do we walk this tricky tightrope? Let's turn to a real-life example:

Four-year-old Clemency is playing with her doll.

Two-year-old Wilbur crawls over and snatches it.

She wails, 'Mummy, he took my toy!'

Then she snarls at him, 'MINE!' and snatches it back.

Wails all round.

You have several tools available to you when a situation like this arises. I go into **SAS** mode. I crouch down, so as not to loom over and trigger another baboon response. I look Clemency in the eyes to engage her while using as few words as I can:

SAY WHAT I SEE

'Clemency, I see you are upset? You're mad because Wilbur took your toy?'

She nods, she calms down quickly because she feels acknowledged and understood.

Wilbur's wailing.

ACKNOWLEDGE

'Wilbur, you wanted the toy?'

He now feels seen and heard, too. I am compassionate with him, for in his mind he just wanted to play. But here comes the boundary: I tell him in as few words as I can, and gently, that he cannot take the toy from his sister.

'You wanted it. But you can't take the toy. Clemency had it.'

He howls loudly. Lessons can be hard to learn! He's upset, but I know I can stay and help him through it. This is an opportunity for me to help him understand an important lesson.

'Wilbur, we don't snatch.'

There is no punishment because Wilbur has done what is normal for a young baboon.

SOOTHE

I soothe him now, because it is a hard lesson for a two-year-old to learn.

'I know it's hard, sweetheart. You really wanted the toy!'

Wilbur also now feels understood. He calms down and looks at me expectantly.

'Clemency, it's okay, sweetheart. You were having such fun with your toy!'

I take Wilbur onto my lap so he feels secure, and then I ask Clemency to see things from Wilbur's perspective.

'Wilbur, can you use your words? Tell Clemency what you wanted?'

Wilbur's teeny owlet brain (that part of his brain that is still developing) shifts into gear. He points to the toy and looks at his sister.

'I want toy.'

'Wilbur wanted to have fun, too, can you see?'

Clemency nods.

She no longer sees her brother as a threat, just an upset little boy. Here we are coaching compassion, so her anger against her brother melts, as she can understand he just wanted to play.

Okay, now the **resolution:**

'Clemency, when you are finished, can you let Wilbur have a turn?'

I am not <u>forcing</u> her to share right now. Sure, I am encouraging her to share, but I give HER the choice of when she does so.

'Wilbur, while you wait, shall we find something fun to do?!'

It can be very difficult for very young children to have to wait their turn, but if we help them with the transition, we can help them experience delayed gratification. We also teach that our world does not end when we don't get our own way.

Wilbur was very happy to play with Mummy, and he quickly found something else fabulous to play with. He could also rest assured that he would still get the toy when Clemency was ready to give it to him. Fifteen minutes later, when Clemency was bored of the toy (and of Mummy playing with Wilbur) she gave him the toy. She actually felt good about giving her brother something she understood he had wanted.

Dr Markham and Nancy Eisenberg are both leading figures in the field of siblings and say children become more generous by having the experience of giving to others and learning how good that feels. If we force them, they feel resentful and quite the opposite – and guess what? They are LESS likely to share after that, too.

So, in this simple but very common scenario, what can we help our children to learn? Wilbur learns:

- I might cry for things but I won't always get my way.
- I can sit and wait my turn without my world falling apart (this is the start of self-regulation).
- It's okay to feel upset, because Mummy will be there to help.
- It feels really good when Clemency finally gives me the toy. I might even have found something better to play with, but my sister has been kind and let me have a turn, and it feels good. I have experienced delayed gratification. (Okay, maybe he doesn't use those *exact* words!)

In time, Wilbur will learn to use his words to ask for a turn. Sometimes his sister might happily oblige, but at other times he might have to wait. Both are okay.

Clemency will learn all the above, too, as the situation will no doubt play out in reverse another time when Wilbur will have something *she* wants to play with. The same ground rules will be applied and she will now have to wait her turn. In addition, Clemency learns:

- Mummy has her back and understands how she feels.
- She can turn to Mummy if there is conflict in future (rather than resorting to hitting).
- That it feels good to give to others.

And that last point is where we start to see the roots of a generosity of spirit borne of a natural positive feedback loop that starts as we help our children to notice other children's feelings and <u>want</u>

to help, rather than feeling forced to do so. All of this has to be a big win-win too for sibling relations!

As your children get older they can be encouraged to use their words more and more so they become better at resolving this type of conflict themselves.

The Family Contract (see Chapter 8) is a great fallback here, too.

For example, in our family contract we have:

- When more than one person wants something, we take turns.
- The person using something decides how long their turn lasts.
- No turn lasts longer than a day.
- If visitors come, we put away really special toys that are hard for us to share.

And so on.

When you have agreed the 'small stuff' and have a clear set of family rules that everyone is on board with, it becomes easier to tackle the bigger issues; for example, birthday gifts: are they exclusive or can the other child play with them if they ask beforehand? Having our children consider the implications and consequences of their actions is a great way to develop that inner wise owl. Clemency once stood firm on birthday presents saying they were hers and hers alone. Wilbur agreed because he said it would be the same for his birthday presents. In reality, when he was given a brilliant lightsabre by my friend Martin, Clemency suddenly wasn't so sure this particular family rule *was* such a great idea! They revisited the contract and then agreed to amend it when

Wilbur negotiated he could play with Clemency's new puppy toy – a win–win that they worked out together. The children drew a present with a bow on the contract, and where it previously read 'Birthday presents are <u>not</u> for sharing', Clemency changed the 'not' to a 'now'!

Don't expect all this to happen like magic. You will know already just how many upsets there are in any given day when you have more than one child. Just take one opportunity each day, if you can, to try to help your children work things through, with your help, to find a win–win solution that they can both live with. You will likely go through this countless times before you see results – but you'll one day find yourself listening to your children animatedly discussing an issue that would previously have caused multiple meltdowns and watch as they draw up a contract between them without so much as a cross word. Yes, it really happens!

2 Sibling aggression and hitting

If our young children feel threatened by a sibling, their immediate instinct might be to lash out. Aggression has its roots in fear. But whereas anger is a valid emotion, we want our children to articulate how they feel in a controlled way, rather than resorting to violence. It takes practice, so don't expect it to happen over-night. But using a Family Contract, Ten-Minute Top-Ups and SAS Parenting, you will help your children graduate to a more sophisticated form of communication, using words over their fists. But what happens when your little baboon is still quicker off the mark?

Let's look at another typical scenario: Clemency smashes Wilbur's Lego tower after he had spent all morning building it. He hits her in frustration. They both come running to me in tears.

Again, we have the **SAS** principle (Say what you see, Acknowledge, Soothe), but we might want to add the idea of not only acknowledging Wilbur's anger but also helping him to direct it in a more appropriate manner.

'I hear shouting and I see two angry people! What happened?'

You don't want to go down the rabbit hole of blame and who did what to whom, but if you are really going to be able to acknowledge both children and understand the upset, you do want to get some sense of what has been going on. Let one child go first, and on another occasion the other can go first.

'Okay, Wilbur, tell me what happened.'

'Clemency smashed my Lego tower!'

'Clemency smashed your Lego tower and you are really mad. I see the Lego on the floor. It is so upsetting when you had built it so high! Clemency, can you tell me what happened?'

'He was being annoying so I smashed it, then he hit me!'

'So, Wilbur was being annoying and you smashed his Lego and then he hit you? I am sorry you are hurt, can you show me?'

I am not taking sides, I am still saying what I see and what I am hearing. I am not trying to do more than understand a little of what has gone on.

Soothe the feelings My priority will be with the child who has been physically hurt first: 'Okay, I can see you are both upset. Wilbur, I need to check Clemency is okay, then I will come to you.' As we talk through what has happened, each child can reflect on what led to this point. Each child has felt heard and each child, as they calm down, is engaged with me to find some solution. I am helping them both regulate and understand the emotions that led to this point.

To find resolution, I might then ask each of them to understand things from the other's perspective, and also to suggest how things might be done differently next time.

For example, when Wilbur was very young (under three), I might've spoken for him:

'Clemency, can you see why Wilbur was cross?'

I encourage her to look at Wilbur, to read his face, his expressions, in order to understand his upset.

I might ask Wilbur to articulate it himself, if he is able to.

'Wilbur, can you tell Clemency with your words why you are cross?'

Then . . .

'Wilbur, you know we have a no-hitting rule. There is no hitting in this house. You cannot hit Clemency. If you cannot use your words, you come and find Mummy, okay?'

I'm sure, like me, you do not want to see one of your children hurt the other, but when physical urges are very present, how best can we get our little baboons to use their words and not resort to hitting each other in the future? We might consider how we can help them to safely expend that 'energy'.

TOOL KIT TIP

Pillow power

We can understand, then, that our very young children might feel compelled to act now and think later, because they have a lizard and baboon brain in charge, motivated by survival, and when under perceived threat, they might 'lash out'. I believe we serve our children better by working with them to help them release their anger safely and appropriately, rather than punishing them, leaving them with pent-up powerful feelings and a tendency to still hit, but to do it when you are not around next time. If we don't address the underlying cause of our children's behaviour, we will not help them, their siblings or ourselves.

With my children, we would *name* the emotion (see Chapter 4), acknowledging that anger is a valid emotion if a child feels they have been wronged. But we want to encourage them to start thinking about how they might express themselves better, more appropriately and safely. I want to be very clear about the boundaries with regard to hitting, so I asked both of them if there was an alternative, something else they felt they could do to express their anger without hitting each other. Wilbur said, 'I could punch a pillow!' I thought this was a rather clever way of him realising that he needed to release the stress – so I enthusiastically picked up a pillow for him to punch. The situation changed very quickly from intense to humorous, as I held up the pillow telling him to give it all he'd got! I realised in this moment that Wilbur had found his own way of releasing the feelings he'd had inside, having been given permission to do so and understanding that it's not anger that's wrong, it is how we express it. (I later referenced this idea with a number of my psychotherapy colleagues, in order to verify its legitimacy.) Over time, Wilbur's need to hit a pillow reduced, as he progressed to using his words.

When our children feel that they are seen and heard, and that their emotions have been validated, we can all move on together to bring about resolution. In this instance, I make sure that Clemency's arm is okay and then encourage some teamwork: 'Okay, come, let's all help build another tower – we can build it even higher!'

The important thing to get from this exchange is that:

- Everyone feels heard.
- Everyone's feelings are acknowledged and validated, which helps with calming things down and ultimately regulating emotions.
- We can understand that we can repair situations (we can rebuild the tower).
- They can come to me for help if this happens again.
- Rather than hit, they can use their words to say, 'I am angry!'

After an incident such as this, you can reinforce the progress by asking them to add a line to the family contract about hitting. In our family, Clemency painted both their palms red and each one pressed a wet palm print onto the paper. Clemency wrote, 'No Hitting!' underneath. We also painted a picture of a tower with a cross through it to emphasise that we must not 'hurt' other people's things, no matter how mad we are.

Rather than judge our children for their explosive outbursts, we should look to help them find an alternative outlet for expressing the big feelings they have inside; for example, choosing pillow power or Star Jumps or a Salsa Shimmy instead. In this way we are helping them to build up that wise owl that will ultimately see them expressing how they feel with words – which in later life will be a jolly good skill to have as grown-ups!

It's unlikely that the outbursts or hitting will stop overnight. When our children are this young it is like a muscle that needs exercising. But each time it happens is an opportunity to help to reiterate the point.

As I say, expect this to take time and a lot of your energy, but trust that it is time and energy well invested. It took me a while with Wilbur, but I knew I had nailed it the night I called home from the BBC newsroom to have Wilbur inform me, 'Mummy, Daddy is getting cross because Clemency is not listening to him,' quickly followed up by, 'He needs to hit a pillow!'

3 Over-assertive siblings

My friend Matthew writes, 'My children are close in age. My son has started to assert his authority with his older sister and, as a consequence, they have started to wind each other up a lot. Whether it is racing each other in the park, who gets to press the elevator button or who sits next to me on the sofa. Whatever this element of competition is, it can quickly turn physical, which I find difficult to witness and resolve (especially if I haven't witnessed the entire spat).'

Siblings will always try to find their place in the pack, as it were. As we have discussed, gender, temperament and an age gap will be a factor in sibling rivalry and how competitive children are likely to be. With boys close in age, it is natural for the youngest to try to assert himself, testing the water, as it were, to see who really is at the top of the pack.

The behaviour Matthew describes is understandable in that context, but clearly it is undesirable if it leads to fighting and upset. So what to do?

Firstly, we might want to consider if the fights are really about the elevator button or who runs the fastest at the park – or whether one child is in need of a little more time-in with Mum or Dad.

If we observe one of our children is constantly in the 'dominant' role, or often the one asserting control over his or her sibling, we will want to address it. We don't want our children to adopt roles and create a family dynamic that can very often end up playing out over the course of their lives. If one child becomes used to winning all the time, he or she might continue to try to exert control and authority over others, while the other sibling might become used to giving in all the time and in later life live out more of a 'victim' role.

If one child appears to have a *need* to control, it will most often be based in insecurity, where he or she feels less in control themselves. We can help our children here simply by allowing them to feel control in other ways. We can do it through play (see Chapter 11) and our special Hero Hours (Chapter 10), which are a great opportunity to give control over to them – to allow them to feel 'all-powerful' and able to boss us around to their heart's content! You can help your child to understand where the boundaries are around control and, ultimately, once they feel more secure to be able to 'give and take'.

For the sibling who has become more used to giving in, we can help them to find their voice. We can encourage our children to use their strong voice and let their sibling know what is and isn't acceptable (helping them, in turn, to lay their own personal boundaries).

Problem solving

Teamwork is super for reducing sibling rivalry and building up wise owls. It teaches our children a valuable life lesson: that there is always repair and also always a solution to be found for any problem. Any time you have a situation, ask your children to find that win–win. When they are really mad at each other, you need first to calm things down.

When our children are calm, we can emphasise the lesson; while everyone is still in a heightened state of arousal, it won't sink in. When your children are calm, then you will see that their little owlet is now engaged and even in charge of that restless baboon. When calm is restored, simply ask them: 'What can we do to resolve the situation?'

After the Lego tower incident, I asked my children what would help them to move forward.

Quick as a flash Clemency said, 'Banish Wilbur from the house!' We were sitting on the floor still, just the three of us, so I smiled and said, 'Okay, that is one solution.'

I picked up a toy from the toy box and said, 'Let's pretend Wilbur is this toy and let's put him over there, away from these three other toys' (representing the three of us).

I then asked Wilbur, 'What would be your solution?'

'Banish Clemency from the house!'

So I put another toy at the other end of where we sat.

'Okay, so now we have both of you outside the "house". Any other solutions?'

Wilbur said, 'Er . . . we could not fight?'

'That sounds like a very good solution – then both of you get to stay in the house!' I added with a smile. 'But how can you not fight?'

'We could come to you?' Wilbur said.

'Or . . . I know,' said Clemency, 'we could use our words and sort it out together.'

'Hmm,' I said (beaming), 'that sounds like a good plan.'

You might want to consider scripts you could keep somewhere handy that are amended to your own situation. You really can keep things simple. Questions like:

- 'Okay so what happened?'
- 'I can see two angry little people – can we take turns to tell Mummy/Daddy what happened?'
- 'What can I do to help?'
- 'What's the solution here?'
- 'What else could we do?'

Remember **SAS** Parenting: say what you see, acknowledge the upset if there is any and then soothe whomever has been 'hurt' or aggrieved. If you have this drawn up in advance of the next alter-cation, you will be ready with some wise owl wisdom and can see what you get back from your children – they might just surprise you!

Apologies

Forcing a child under three or even four to 'say sorry' is not really going to solve the problem. Remember, the wise owl brain only really 'gets online' (as Dr Bruce Perry puts it) at around the age of three, and even then it's still very much a work in progress. It is the wise owl brain that is in charge of understanding right from wrong and of having a strong sense of morality. Of course, this is what we want to instil in our children and we might start to do this and build their fluffy owlet up, but forcing them to apologise will not do that. It only works if your child genuinely FEELS sorry for what they have done and therefore feels a natural urge to want to say sorry. When that happens, you will see the empathy in their eyes when they look at the person and say 'sorry'. They have to *feel* it, or else, there is little point.

We want our children to be genuine and authentic in their engagement with others, so this is where we must 'wise owl' it and trust our children to WANT to say sorry if they have hurt some-one's feelings. It is the same for us as adults. We can only really be sorry for our actions if we can acknowledge that we have done something that has hurt or upset others. To do that we must *feel* the hurt of the other person – have empathy with them. Consider how easy you find it to genuinely say sorry and you'll also know this can sometimes take real courage. This is why we want to help our children to have a strong sense of self, in order that, in saying sorry, they don't feel bad about themselves. They can simply own up to their behaviour, honestly and authentically, knowing that the world will not end when they do.

If we punish our young children and force them to apologise (or send out notes to other children at a later date, as some parents do), I am not sure we are really helping with that.

By raising your children with empathy and compassion they will naturally become empathetic and compassionate adults. Then, if they can feel what it is like to be in someone else's shoes, they will automatically want to say sorry. The same as we might say sorry as parents – so they will model us, all in good time.

So, for now, for under-fives I would instead say to my children:

'Look at your brother's face. How does he look to you?'

'Sad.'

'And do you understand why he is sad?'

'Because I hurt him.'

Again, don't expect this always to go to plan, and remember, with a baboon brain in charge, your child might be on too much of an overload to really stop and take stock.

As long as you have tried – and you keep trying – and as long as the hurt or injured sibling feels you have really understood their hurt and have acknowledged it, then you can find some resolution.

* * *

The single most frequently asked question about sibling rivalry is: how can we stop the squabbling and raise lifelong friends?

The simplest answer is: YOU.

Over time the dynamic will shift with your support, and your siblings will work as a team. The key words are: 'YOUR SUPPORT'.

The more you fill your child's emotional cup, the more those anxious feelings and fears about who you love most, whom you would save first if the house was on fire, will subside, because each child feels 'loved enough'.

When we understand our children's *fear* (and any resulting un-desirable behaviour) stems from a need to feel close to you, we can see why we are so crucial to solving sibling rivalry.

As I have stressed throughout this book, *the time you invest in these first five years will be time very well invested.*

Wise Owl Wisdoms

- Sibling rivalry is a natural consequence of evolution.
- Acknowledge and understand it can create real feelings of unease, sometimes even unconsciously.
- When your children feel 'loved enough', and have enough of you, the rivalry should lessen.
- With your support, you can raise siblings who become friends for life.
- Always be your child's Squabble Stopper!

Sibling rivalry can often seem like a complex dance that your children will do day in and day out. You will have many oppor-tunities to help them navigate their way through, and trust that, age, gender and temperament aside, and with your help as the Squabble Stopper-in-Chief, you really can help your children become firm friends for life!

CHAPTER 13

Big Life Changes, Childcare and Starting School

'Hugs can change the World.'

DR GUDDI SINGH, Integrated
Child Health Quality Improvement
Fellow and Paediatric Registrar

One cold September morning I was sitting on a wooden bench, nursing my three-month-old son. I was surrounded by wet raincoats and brightly coloured miniature wellington boots that were covered in the mud from the field through which the children had splashed on their walk to school. I huddled under my own warm coat and held my son close to me while he fed, his snuffling mews coming up from beneath the material.

'Mummy are you still here,' cried a little girl in pigtails as she ran in from the room next door. She wore a blue-and-white gingham over-shirt that fell below her knees. She was not yet three years old. My heart swelled.

'Hello, darling, Mummy is right here'.

Clemency turned and ran back into the melee of a classroom of toddlers sitting among blocks, building towers and reading books. Another ten minutes and she was back, the blonde bobbed hair swinging through just before she did. 'Hello again, Mummy!' she sang. She smiled at me, ran over to pat Wilbur on the head and ran off again. It was day five of my daughter's September start at pre-school. I had already spent three long, cold mornings in that boot room. I felt ridiculous at times; I should have been at home with my young son in the warm. But after the first terrible morning with Clemency screaming for me not to leave her, I had been torn. My husband and I had reassured ourselves it was the right time to send our daughter to pre-school given she was nearly three, but with hindsight I realised the arrival of a new baby brother had made it far from ideal.

Traditionally, in our society, three years old is considered an appropriate time for our toddlers to attend nursery. Experience shows us that around this time the baboon is keen to encourage physical independence and is much more social. With a new baby in the house, however, that baboon of Clemency's was torn between having fun with some newfound freedom and having serious FOMO (fear of missing out), given the imposter of a baby brother had arrived and threatened to take Mum's attentions away!

The nursery staff tried to reassure me that 'She'll be fine, she'll stop crying after you leave', but having my child taken from my arms when she was crying for me broke my heart and, after day one, I couldn't do it again. I asked if I could stay with my daughter until she was more settled. I worried I would be seen as somehow difficult or an over-sensitive mum and found it hard to know what was best, so I sought advice from psychotherapist Liza Elle:

'Why would anyone want to take your child from you when they are in distress?' Liza asked me gently. 'And why wouldn't she be in distress? [In this instance] she has just lost you to a baby brother and now you want to leave her in a place that's unfamiliar to her. Consider, too, that she has no real concept of time yet, which means she's unsure when or even *if* you will be coming back.' Liza fixed me with a look that was at once both kind yet firm.

I sat in silence. I finally understood. If we, as adults, would find that situation tough to deal with, what must it be like for our children?

* * *

Loss and change are important and universal concepts, so it's critically important for us to understand the impact they have on our children, especially when they are very young.

For starters, science tells us that the stress of separation between a parent and a young child is experienced in the brain in much the same way as physical pain. This is the emotion of LOSS that we now know can trigger a whole-body stress response. Our children will certainly experience some big life events that will include loss and change, sometimes on a daily basis throughout these early years: that might be divorce, death or their best friend moving away, and certainly something as significant as starting nursery or school for the first time. Even what can seem like a positive event, as we become excited about our little ones gaining some degree of independence, can, to them, feel like a VERY BIG EMOTIONAL EXPERIENCE. How we mark that occasion with them will directly affect how positively our child experiences that event and will shape their response to similar events in the future.

We're going to look now at how we can HELP support our

children through these inevitable transitions, with their lizard and baboon brain in mind, to enable them to adapt, to be flexible, and ultimately to become resilient, even if and when at first things feel a little testing. Let's dismiss any fears that our young children might be 'clingy' if they express a need to be close to us. Being clingy has such a negative connotation, but in fact it simply means our children might feel unsafe at that moment and have the *need* to cling to us, just as nature intended – just look at the animal kingdom for proof.

So, regardless of whether it is you popping away from your baby to the kitchen momentarily, or the opposite end of the spectrum when you are taking your child to nursery or school for the first time, please rest assured that if your child finds it hard to bear parting from you, they are simply saying, 'I don't feel safe' and able to 'go it alone' right now. That's fine – they simply need a bit more support. With your help, with you being there for them in these moments of anxiety, you are <u>more</u> likely to see your child grow in confidence and able to go it alone, once that lizard and baboon feel more assured.

In all these varied transitions in their young lives, if our children are left alone in distress, with cortisol and adrenaline flooding their bodies, and without us to help bring them back to balance, that's not good at all, as we saw in Chapter 2. Few of us like change, whether it's moving house, changing jobs, or losing someone we love. However, WE are able to rationalise that the stress of moving house won't last forever, that we will soon settle into our new jobs, that we can find friends with whom we can talk about our loss and find comfort in our grieving, knowing 'this too will eventually pass'. But our children, and especially babies and very young children, CANNOT! If they are left to 'cope' alone and in distress during times of great change or transition, the truth is they are not coping.

With all this in mind, let's take a look at some of the major transitions your children under the age of five might face, and how your understanding of their lizard, baboon and wise owlet brains will enable you to help them through these experiences with compassion and understanding, which in turn will help them build resilience and, in time, their own mature and well-balanced wise owl.

Early separation

A baby cannot yet talk or express how they feel in words, so it is absolutely vital that parents understand that how we help babies through transitions is crucial to their future emotional well-being. Perhaps one of the most common frustrations of any parent of a newborn is that, 'I can't even leave the room without the baby screaming for me!'

Even short separations from us can be stressful for our young children. The lizard and baboon are all about survival and at certain stages of development, a separation from the person they depend on for their safety can trigger a stress response even during what seems a very brief absence. Our babies and toddlers don't have a fully developed sense of time, remember, so even short separations can trigger anxiety because how are they to know how long it will be before we return? Our babies and toddlers can sense and *feel* our absence. In understanding that, we can respond to our babies' distress in these moments and perhaps simply take them with us!

This is not about your child being 'weak' or 'clingy', rather they are at a period in their development when they feel unsafe without you there. Again, this is all part of them having that ancient brain and behaving as Nature designed! Remember that lizard needs reassurance that you can be trusted to be there – and to come back. In other words, to not abandon him. But if we do need to be parted for longer periods, for example when/if we return to work, Liza Elle advised preparing for the separation, which led to me using the tool I call the Boomerang Bye-Bye.

TOOL KIT TIP

Boomerang Bye-Bye

When my children were very young, Liza advised me, 'Even *before* you return to work, start building up a ritual to allow the children to know you will be "coming back".' When you leave the room temporarily, even just to go to the loo, tell them that, "Mummy's coming back'. Even when you think they are too young to understand you. Simply say, "Mummy's coming back" each time you go. And when you walk back in the room, starting after a separation of just a minute or so, you say brightly, "Mummy's back!"'

Liza states this is setting up a pattern of security, a little ritual, something they can depend upon, because children cannot tell the time or have a clear concept of 'how long' you might be gone for. Over time, when they hear, 'Mummy's coming back,' they will start to settle, understanding from those early days post-birth that that means she WILL come back.

This idea extends to when you start to leave the house without your young child, perhaps in the care of a child-minder, relative or friend: those very early, tentative steps outside without your precious little one, even for just a short period. Old-school parenting often advised leaving our children without saying goodbye, because it was thought that if we did tell our child we were leaving, it would 'upset them'. This is – again – where I say old-school parenting was misguided. If we leave our children without telling them we are going, it not only upsets them but it also destabilises their lizard and baboon, putting them on edge because the person they thought they could trust simply ups and leaves. In building up little rituals, in being consistent with our 'goodbyes', our children <u>will</u> build the flexibility and the capacity to cope. But if we sneak out of the house (and, later, the nursery) without saying goodbye, it can do quite the reverse.

Children aged one to three years

Once your child is beyond the newborn stage, our adult lives will inevitably start to impact on when and how we need to be away from our young children, whether that is with babysitters, relatives or, naturally, childcare and education. I will touch on the latter towards the end of this chapter, but for now please know that there are really helpful techniques we can use that can help to ease the stress of the transition and/or the separations our children might have to endure.

TOOL KIT TIP

Referencing

When we understand that our children's natural attachment to us WILL make it difficult for them to be parted from us, we can feel confident to soothe their uncertainty and know they will transition far more smoothly with our help and support rather than without it. We should not leave our children to simply 'sink or swim', they need our help with transitions not to have to go it alone. Back at the nursery, I spoke with the nursery lead and explained that with a new baby in the mix I felt my daughter might need a bit of extra help in transitioning to spending time away from home and, most importantly at that point, me. I asked if I could stay for a few days to help her settle. They agreed, but the only space they said was available was in that cold, dank boot room. I took it. I took it because I felt strongly it was important for Clemency to have me there and for her to be able to find security through what is known as 'referencing', where a child is introduced to a situation with Mum, Dad or her primary carer, in her presence. She is encouraged to 'go play', but with her attachment figure close by, so she can come and go – and reference them – to know they are there if she needs them. It's this that can so quickly build up a child's confidence, because very soon they establish that this new territory is safe. Their baboon then takes over, keen as she is for her independence and play, and once she trusts the people inside the new camp to keep her safe too, then, bingo, Mum's not as necessary to have there any more!

When we talk about referencing, we might consider traditional communities again. Children who are securely attached to their parents from birth will gradually seek more and more independence naturally. They follow that atavistic baboon urge to be curious, to make friends and to explore. It is part of their emotional and physical development. In more traditional cultures, children would have access to more than a dozen adults and other children during the course of the day, and will still run back to their parents at intervals throughout. *Our children might live in the modern world, but they still have ancient brains.* THAT'S why our pre-school children need the transition time: to help them feel safe in a new camp that is far away from Mum and/or Dad. They need to trust that this new 'camp' (the nursery) is safe and that they have someone nearby (their new teacher) whom they can trust for support. This is why we have a key person in nursery settings now. Until our children find that security with a teacher/ key figure they can feel attached to, they want to be able to know that Mum or Dad is close by.

Each morning I explained to Clemency that Mummy would stay in the little room until, and unless, she felt happy for me to leave. I assured her I would stay in the boot room, that the door would be open and she could come and see me whenever she needed to. Each morning during the course of that first week, she would run back and forth between the two rooms, clearly just checking I was still there. Excited and engaged by the activity going on in the other room, she would then happily run straight back in, once she had seen I was. This back and forth went on for a few more days before I told her I was going to go for a coffee and would come back in a little while. 'You're coming back?' she asked hesitantly. 'Yes, darling, Mummy's coming back'. She stood for a moment longer than usual, then, 'Okay, see you soon, Mummy!' and ran off again.

The relief I felt was enormous. I made my way down the wooden steps of the nursery for what I imagined would be the final time to have a coffee (I swear I could see the relief on the teacher's faces as they saw me go, too) and I came back half an hour later for pick-up. Clemency was so excited to see me and chatted all the way home about the things she had done while I had been 'gone'.

That was the last day Clemency asked me to stay. She had made the transition. She was happy. I was delighted. It was all good.

Children over three

As children start to gain more independence, and that baboon is urging them to experience new things, it can still help to have a transitional object to keep you connected in spirit, even if you are not there in person.

TOOL KIT TIP

Pebble in the pocket

Your child might already have a special toy they carry around with them as a form of comfort. If they are starting school or a new school and they say they want to have it with them, perhaps you might speak with the school to see if it is possible for your child to bring it for the first week in their bag, just to help them with the transition. Don't worry that they will then always need it – it is better to take notice of the need and seek to understand where it is coming from. If your child is clearly in need of more emotional security, then it is a sign for YOU to help support them through this period of change.

Your investment in your child now will be far more precious to them than anything else. Perhaps you could also ask to work with the school to find other ways to help your child with this period of change, rather than seeing that it is something 'wrong'. It might be that they can allocate a teacher to her so that while you are your child's 'rock' and support at home this particular teacher becomes your child's 'rock' at school. Again, this won't have to be forever, once your child is feeling more secure and has made firm friends, the need for the teacher will dissipate but it's better to do it this way than expect your child to have to cope alone.

If your child does not already have a 'special' toy, then in the run-up to them starting school you might see what you can find together during your one-hour special time – a small pebble perhaps, or another object that you have been playing with. The simple idea is that when it becomes something they associate with you, they might find it reassuring to take it in to school with them in their bag for the first day. It then becomes almost as if they are taking something of you with them for security. My friend Rosie drew a small heart on her little boy's wrist when he first went to school and he then drew one on hers. They continue to do this as he grows older and she tells me that it gives her as much comfort as it gave him on his first few days of school.

This is a lovely idea to help your children through any separation from you – whether it is staying with Granny for the first time or you are going on a date night for a few hours. Having an object, a toy or even an item of clothing can help your child to still feel connected with you.

All children

Ensuring our children feel connected to us – whatever age they are – will help act as a buffer to any wobbles they might have in your absence.

TOOL KIT TIP

Rituals

Rituals, as we have discussed with the **BOOMERANG BYE-BYE**, can be a wonderful way to build up confidence, as they give that little baboon some certainty in a time that perhaps feels a little LESS certain. Having a ritual that you share can really help: something special that the two of you can share to help your child last the day without you, knowing that you have something that binds you both together.

'The most important factor in the child's experience [of nursery/childcare] is a positive and warm attachment [to a key person]. Understanding children's idiosyncrasies, remembering their comforters, figuring out their little parting rituals is essential to harmonious relationships. My daughter needed to wave out the window to me before she turned her back and enjoyed the day with her friends. This was new to the nursery but they found a step so she could reach and stood with her until I walked out the gate. We introduced this into some of our nurseries as she isn't alone in needing a leaving ritual. My son, had to have *The Old Lady Who Swallowed A Fly* read in its entirety every day! Nurseries which are not flexible or empathetic to the needs of parent and child may not be the best ones.'

June O'Sullivan MBE, CEO of the London Early Years Foundation

For Wilbur, when he first started school, we came up with a little song, '*I love you, you love me, I'll come back for you at three.*' We sang it on the way to school and it was his way of knowing that I would be coming back and he could get a sense that at three o'clock it was home time. Songs and anything rhythmic is good, as we learned with Dr Bruce Perry on page 108, for soothing that dorsal vagus nerve – the lizard. The rhythm of things can literally rhythm out (iron out) the worries in their heads (and ours).

Starting nursery and/or school

Let's say a friend invites you to a party. She drives you there, as it's in a part of town that you aren't familiar with. Your friend is excited, she seems to know EVERYONE, but you don't know a single soul. You tell her you're nervous and not sure you'll enjoy it, but she hushes you and says it will be fine. When you arrive, the place is PACKED and the music is so LOUD that you can't hear what anyone's saying. Your adrenaline surges and you're not sure you want to stay. Your friend gives you a hug and says she's leaving. She nudges you towards some-one who pulls you into the crowd. You look back, but she's gone . . . and you feel a sense of panic. You don't know when or if your friend is coming back and you don't know how to get home.

Now imagine what your young child might feel like on their first day at nursery and/or school.

Starting school represents a massive rite of passage for us as parents, as well as our children. We might experience a combination of nervousness as well as excitement on behalf of our growing baboons, and that is most likely similar to how they will feel, too. You might find your child is more anxious than you had anticipated. Remember, there is nothing wrong with 'clingy' or anxious, perhaps your son or daughter had a tricky start at nursery and that memory is now lodged in their baboon's memory sack. Whatever the reason, it is simply important to acknowledge and honour your child with their upset and not try to dismiss it with a, 'Oh, you'll be fine!' or, 'Come on, be a big boy/girl now!'

The whole-body stress response in childcare and primary-school settings has been recorded by a number of studies, which have concluded that children in these settings exhibit higher cortisol levels than children at home. That might make for uncomfortable reading, but it is a fact we are all wise to understand, especially if we are driven to 'drop and go' because we don't (understandably) want to see our children in distress, but we – and indeed anyone caring for children – do well to be aware of the potential consequences of that.

Georgia Robinson, clinical director, Kent Well-Being Hub, told me that, 'Understanding our own distress when leaving our children is important. The temptation to avoid our upset is disguised as "not wanting to upset the child". I have witnessed this time and time again in schools when teachers are leaving their jobs and feel it is better to not mention to the children because they do not want to upset them. What they are in reality doing is avoiding the pain and upset of the child, because they won't be there to see it when the children return. But then, of course, the child is having to deal with not only the loss of a teacher but also the added feelings of not being worthy enough or important enough to say goodbye to and can bring up feelings of abandonment.'

It's an important point that Georgia Robinson raises. Few of us find it easy to sit with someone else's pain – not least our children's.

But we do ourselves and our children greater service when we are able to sit with our children in these moments, to acknowledge it might feel 'painful' and to reassure them we are coming back. As I have already explained, babies and very young children will find it hard to achieve the 'emotional magic' of emotional regulation all by themselves. They *will* be distressed when we leave them in the care of others, because Nature designed them to be, and they will need help to return to emotional balance if their natural 'stress response' is triggered.

I have spoken with so many parents who say they feel dreadful when they leave their children in grave distress at the school gates. Some say they feel forced to override their own natural instincts because they either find it too painful to witness (as Georgia highlights) or else they feel embarrassed and have that old, 'Is there something wrong with me or my child?' guilt thing going on. Nope ... I'm not having that for you! And if you doubt me, let me send in Mike to lend a military hand!

 ## Man-ouevres with Mike

'Being calm under pressure when surrounded by other parents (and teachers!) can be a challenge. I have found that it helps enormously to learn to separate yourself totally from your surroundings and any judgements you think are being made about you. What does it matter what they think? Concentrate fully on your child and what might be causing their upset; don't worry about the upset you might be causing to others. I have experienced it, so I do know how it feels, whether it's the school queue, the supermarket or on a plane – I can tell just by the look on someone's face if they have or have not got children. If they don't, it's more an annoyed look of "Can't you control your child?" (to which the answer might have been no!). It differs from the look of someone who is a parent who has that empathy, mostly, "You poor bast**d" and relief they are not in your situation!

'Ultimately, though, for any stressful situation you find yourself in, I find taking three deep breaths in and out really helps, because if YOU'RE not calm, you haven't a snowball-in-hell's chance of calming your child. And again, as Kate says, and as I in fact say when I'm training, 'If it feels wrong, it IS wrong.' Trust your instincts, they are there for a reason: to keep you – and your child – safe.'

We are designed to comfort our children if they cry, not to have them snatched from our arms (as I have seen happen too many times) while our children are screaming for us. This sort of practice serves to undermine trust between you and your child, and unsettles the lizard and baboon, leaving your child 'out of kilter' emotionally. I think this practice of whisking children away at the gate has been influenced by an old-school worry that if a child is 'indulged', they will become MORE 'clingy' and never want to leave their parent's side. But it's quite the reverse. When we take a little more time to comfort and calm our children, the more capable and competent emotionally they become. As we know now from the science, when we can build up the strongest foundations for our children at the start of their lives, the more secure their attachment with us, the more reassured the lizard and baboon become. This is what builds resilience and the capacity for separation, rather than the opposite!

So, PLEASE never let anyone *tell* you your child is 'too clingy', or that it is acceptable to wrench your children from you when they are crying. Why would they want you to go against what Nature designed?!

Quality childcare settings led by many excellent early years specialists will be very aware of all this and go to great lengths to mitigate and alleviate our children's 'separation distress'. The topic of choosing the right nursery and school for you and your child, is HUGE and obviously justifies a separate discussion outside the remit of my book; not for no reason are there literally hundreds of books dedicated to the subject, some of which I will highlight in the Resources section at the back of this book. A good source of information on this topic is June O'Sullivan's book *The A to Z of Early Years: Politics, Pedagogy and Plain Speaking* (see page 296).

That said, with specific practicalities of your life and circumstances aside, the tools above will, I hope, give you a number of options to help your children through any challenging times, as they enter the world of childcare and education.

TOOL KIT TIP

Be you, be human!

It really helps your child to know that you get nervous about big events, too. Knowing that whatever they are feeling about the change or event is normal helps them to 'come through it'. If they know that EVEN Mum or Dad gets nervous, it will help to normalise the feeling even further. You don't have to be invincible in these moments, for example, by saying something like 'Well, I NEVER get nervous, so you shouldn't either.' You are already invincible in your child's eyes. But if you can show vulnerability and still remain strong, you teach your child an incredibly valuable lesson. It is okay to be vulnerable – there is strength in that because we can always overcome it.

Your child will think: *Wow, if Dad gets nervous or makes a mistake, it's okay for me to do so too!* Adding a fun story here can also be helpful, as humour will help to diffuse any anxiety. I usually tell a story where I get nervous and trip up in front of everyone or even fart (I clearly do not fart, that's always the puppy) or something equally silly that makes the children laugh and helps to promote that wonderful feel-good hormone oxytocin and those amazing natural opioids.

* * *

Bereavement

If there is a bereavement in, or close to, the family, it can take a while for your children to process. They might keep coming back to 'so Daddy won't be here any more', or 'Why did Grandma have to die?' It might feel like the twentieth time you've had the same conversation, but that just means your child is simply having difficulty working it through, and this is helping them to do it. Don't get exasperated or irritable. I appreciate if someone has died, then the questions can feel quite triggering and you might find yourself responding with less wise owl and more baboon, in which case you might simply explain to your child, 'I am sorry to snap, but Mummy is sad, too, and I think I need a jolly good cry!'

Parent ponders: Tony, dad to two young boys

'I lost my dad to a very rare form of dementia, and at a young age. My two boys had very few years of Grandad being well enough to play with them. When he finally passed, after nearly 15 years of, at times, very traumatic care, I came back from the home and had to break the news to my two. I knew they would be upset, so I prepared myself to also

show my feelings, and not "be strong" and silent. I said that Grandad's body had stopped working so well and he had died.

'They both burst into tears.

'I got upset, too.

'I just sat with them and hugged them, we cried together, they asked me questions and I did my best to answer them. Eventually, the youngest fell asleep on me and the eldest sat there holding my hand for the longest time.

'I immediately began helping them come to terms with the loss of their beloved Grandad as best I could. I showed them photos and told them funny stories of his footballing days, of when he used to have old cars that he repaired and would always laugh and bang spanners when it all went wrong – they laughed and I laughed. I sat with them and I held their hands, still.

'Now they are older, they still miss their Grandad, of course they do – they always will. But they can cry or laugh when they feel it is right for them. They understand that life has cycles and they know that the memories of Grandad will never go away. Understanding transitions in your child's life is so important, because there will be so many, and Kate's advice is absolutely life-changing for these challenging moments.'

Remember to name the emotions your child might be experiencing, not to be afraid of them. Child bereavement charities are excellent places to start looking for support in helping your child if it is a very difficult time. The key is that children feel they have you, even if they cannot readily express how they are feeling, knowing you are there can be soothing and healing enough. So long as you remain responsive and show that you see them in their distress.

You might want to make a box of things with reminders of the person who has died, or reminders of friends or memories they have had when you were all together. You can use rituals for being able to say goodbye to a loved one or a place. You could make a song or a card; ask your child how THEY want to remember someone or what THEY want to do to mark the experience.

Remember not to dismiss your child's emotions, and recognise that you may have to work harder if this is a period of hurt or distress for you, too. If we are recently bereaved, we have our own needs, but remember that your child does not have a fully grown wise owl yet, you still need to be a wise owl for them and put those wonderful warm wings around them during periods of change. (In the Resources section I have included a list of helpful organisations, including Place2Be.)

Loss

Loss is not just when someone passes away. Loss is an intense feeling for our children, and one that will unite many of the experiences they will have during this period of their lives. It's another area where our children might need our help in order to build emotional resilience and regulation. If a relative is extremely poorly, if you are going through a divorce, if you are changing your childcarer or job, or even if you are planning to move house, you will need to consider how to prepare your child for the inevitable upset that the 'loss' will entail.

Sadly, we cannot spare our children pain. Hardship is an inevitable part of life. How you help them in this period will define how well they deal with pain throughout the rest of their life, so it is REALLY important that you don't try do anything artificially in order to spare their tears . . . they will only come further down the line, or else see your child stuffing their emotions down into that emotional rucksack and it will weigh them down.

> **Brain Box** 'Don't worry about hiding your feelings, if you're worried or concerned about something – sharing how you feel helps your child feel safe, and enables them to share how they feel. Reassure them that it's okay to feel the way they do; it can help if you do an activity while they are talking, or have a feelings jar where they can write their feelings down.'
>
> Merle Davies, NSPCC (Director, Centre for Early Child Development)

TOOL KIT TIP

'I need to P!'

No, not THAT kind of pee – I am talking about PREPARATION! My husband Mike had this idea drilled into him when he was in the Marines. The military call it 'Prior preparation prevents p*ss poor performance' but perhaps you might want to avoid that when talking to the main nursery lead at Busy Bees.

Unlike some transitions, such as bereavement or illness, many big changes are scheduled, they have a time frame: we KNOW they are going to happen. When this is the case, **YOU NEED TO P!** Involve and prepare your children well in advance for a transition that you know is approaching. Firstly, having that all-important conversation that, for example, you are considering, or going to be, moving house or school, or that one parent is moving out. Try to have these conversations as early as possible, once you are certain what is likely to happen.

You might drip-feed the information into conversations using age-appropriate questions. Let's use the BIG CHANGE of moving house as an example:

'So we have been looking at a new place to live. We are think-ing about X.'

You can sit down and show your children photos. Include them in the conversation about the area the new house is in, and per-haps suggest a day trip to see it.

Understand this might feel difficult, and deploy SAS Parenting (see page 90) so you can acknowledge it and help to soothe any fears.

Don't dismiss the worries or fears. Acknowledge your child might be worried about making new friends or leaving old ones behind.

Explain your reasons for doing so, in order that your child knows there is a REASON for the move and that you have had to think it through carefully.

Normalise it as much as you can, to make it part of the every-day conversations, and encourage your child to ask questions as often as possible.

Involve your children in as much decision-making as you can: what colour to paint their bedroom, where the new dog bed will go, or where to put their favourite toys, anything to make things easier starting at the new school – more play dates maybe?

Ask THEM questions to engage their fluffy owlet brain so that they can rationalise and soothe their own lizard and baboon in the process, considering the positives of the big 'change', rather than worry about 'what the negatives might be'.

Use time frames if your child has a good grasp of the concept, otherwise try to work out a way that they can get a sense of when it might be. Is it happening around Christmastime, or when they finish school or after a holiday, for example?

Find a positive way to mark the event so they can look forward or prepare for it. You might want to put a calendar on the wall to check off the days.

Use creative outlets – make a photo book of all the times you have spent at your old house, including family holidays and school friends. Encourage your child to be creative when they feel wobbly, doing lots of play to help them express how they feel on paper. Or perhaps a bit of pillow power (page 232) if need be!

You might want to use art to draw or paint what a new house might look like (or the house of your partner if they are moving out). You can discuss what that might look like, use colours and descriptions so they really get a sense of this change happening, of it 'coming alive', as it were. If you are divorcing or separating, your child might want to sit with your partner and draw what their new house will look like, and although I can appreciate this might take all your inner resolve to sit and watch, it is important to do so especially with painful endings like divorce. Children's feelings can often get lost in the adult pain that is swirling around.

Ask your child how <u>they</u> might want to mark the change that is approaching. You might want to encourage them to plan and signify the ending, perhaps by drawing a timeline, or you can also ask how it sits in their body. Have them make a collage or something creative to let you know how they are feeling. You might notice they draw with darker colours – that's okay. Be led by your child, don't assume anything, don't comment on what they have drawn. Resist the urge to say things like 'Oh, that's really black, you must be really sad.' Feel confident you can allow them the process of grieving the change or loss, which is what they may effectively be doing in these moments.

Do all these things together with your child. By allowing them a safe space to release any worries or hurt, they can literally lay their feelings bare on the page. Don't feel the need to analyse – just by allowing them this process and being there with them is helping them to release any upset in a deep and profound way.

* * *

In addition to all of these ideas, I would like to make a few points that are well worth considering in order for you to always be mindful of the lizard, baboon and their little owlet, and to see these BIG LIFE MOMENTS through the eyes of your little ones:

Don't expect too much, too soon They are young lizards and baboons, they need time to adjust, to process what is going on, to feel safe and to understand why the world they previously knew seems to have suddenly changed. When we don't force our children, when we take a few days rather than expecting them to feel 'safe' instantly, the transition is likely to be smooth and successful.

Ensure your children feel SEEN and HEARD and that you are thinking/have thought all this through with them in mind.

Take responsibility for what is happening Sometimes children can blame themselves for whatever is happening. A common scenario is that children might blame themselves for a big change such as parents separating, thinking it was because they did something wrong.

Let your children experience the gift of crying when they are upset. Don't shut them down and say, 'Oh, don't cry or you will make me upset, too.' It is GOOD to cry, remember? Tears cleanse the soul, as they say, both yours and your child's. If they cry, you know it is their hurt being released. Crying in these difficult moments enables them to find both comfort *and* resolution, and by doing it WITH you, the bond between you gets strengthened and healing can take place.

BE A WISE OWL! When you speak with warmth and real empathy – trying to put yourself in your child's shoes, understanding that this might be triggering their lizard and baboon if it feels scary, and being prepared to simply sit with them – you are helping them to build up their own inner wise owl, which will serve them well in the future.

FINALLY, during times of great change, don't forget the other tools you have in your kit. SAS Parenting will be super-useful: Say What You *See*, Acknowledge and then Soothe. Here are a few words that might be useful depending on what transition or change you are all facing:

1 SAY WHAT YOU SEE/HEAR
'It seems that this may feel a bit difficult.'

'It seems that you are not keen . . . I can understand that . . . '

'I am sensing some sadness around this . . . would you like to have a cuddle and a chat?'

2 ACKNOWLEDGE
'I imagine it might feel very hard right now and that's okay. It *is* hard.'

'What is it that you will miss the most? What is it that you find most difficult?'

'Change is difficult. I understand that. It can make us feel wobbly inside.'

Acknowledge their pain and yours, too, if you are sad:

'I understand it is painful to think about Grandma dying. Mummy/Daddy is sad about it, too.'

'I understand you are sad about me leaving to live in another house. I understand you will miss me. I will miss you, too.'

3 SOOTHE
'I am here, and we will get through this together.'

'I am with you, I am not going anywhere.'

Also, I must refer you back to your fantastic **TEN-MINUTE TOP-UPS** (on page 178), which will top up your child's 'emotional cup' each day before your child starts school (or before any big transition or life event). In practice, this often just sees me filling up their emotional cup before school, having body-to-body contact, sitting on the **SOOTHING STAIR** (page 155), to help bring those cortisol levels down and calm the stress response. We might sit and read a book or sometimes sit hugging, me rocking back and forth knowing that it is those cuddles again helping to regulate and 'repair' any worries or fears.

You also have **Code Reds** (page 134) for your child to express their worries after time away from you, plus you have **STOP SN-O-T**, too, to allow you to get that all-important perspective and ability to dive in and help them.

And during the build-up to any big transition, always remember your one **HERO HOUR** (page 183) a week is also vital (as well as those ten minutes a day). The more connected your child feels to you in the weeks ahead of any big event, the better prepared they will feel, because they have a strong sense of you being there 'no matter what'.

Life is constantly in motion and we will always have a need to adapt to change. We can acknowledge that change is often unsettling for us all. For our children, with their young lizard, baboon and fluffy owlets, these changes can be very alarming. However, when our children know they have someone they trust by their side for any transition, no matter how big or small, it helps to sustain them through any anxious periods and builds resilience – something they will certainly need if they are to cope better with the knocks and challenges life will certainly throw their way later on.

* * *

By adding **Boomerang Bye-Byes, Referencing** and **Pebble in your Pocket** as well as **Rituals, Be Human**, and **I Need to P!**, you now have a Tool Kit brimming with ideas to help you and your children through ANY transition. Further, when added to all the other tools I have talked about in my book, there is NOTHING that you cannot cope with, no situation where you will be at a loss as to what to do and no challenge that you cannot dive into and turn around for your child. By being your child's super-hero, deploying all these tools and understanding how their lizard, baboon and wise owl affect their behaviour, you will be able to transform their lives and make your own experience of parenting as joyful and rewarding as it can be.

Whatever the storm, you've got this!

Wise Owl Wisdoms

ᴠ ᴠ Loss and change are inevitable in life. It's critically important for us to understand the impact they have on our
children, especially when they are very young.

ᴠ ᴠ The stress of separation between a parent and a young
child can be experienced in the brain in much the same
way as physical pain.

ᴠ ᴠ If your child is 'clingy' or anxious about you leaving, they
are simply telling you they don't feel safe.

ᴠ ᴠ When we support our children in their moments of anxiety we
help to <u>build</u> confidence and resilience, rather than the reverse.

ᴠ ᴠ Our children can adapt and cope with change when they
have our help and support.

ᴠ ᴠ Few of us like change or to see our children in distress – but
staying with them, acknowledging the pain of the experience and guiding them through will help them enormously.

ᴠ ᴠ When we take a little more time to comfort and calm our
children, the more capable and competent emotionally
they become.

ᴠ ᴠ In choosing childcare, if it 'feels wrong', it is wrong – trust
your instincts and find carers who have empathy and
share your 'wise owl' view.

ᴠ ᴠ Be you, be honest (as much as your child's age allows) –
you are more powerful than you know.

CHAPTER 14

We Cannot Pour
From an Empty Cup

'I would rather be the child of a mother
who has all the inner conflicts of the human
being than be mothered by someone for
whom all is easy and smooth, who knows
all the answers and is a stranger to doubt.'

DONALD WINNICOTT,
English paediatrician and psychoanalyst

OMG, we got here!

I mean, I got to finish my book . . . and you got to read it to the end!

Both of us with young children and juggling ten different plates,
no doubt . . . well done us!

My husband Mike, as you know, is a former Royal Marines

commando. He used to joke that if parenthood was a ship, it would be called HMS Relentless. It's true, we are never 'off' when we are parents. Being a parent IS challenging, especially if and when we find ourselves parenting solo.

It's not a cliché to say parenting is the toughest job going. It is even tougher when our own 'emotional cup' is half empty.

We cannot expect to parent well when we ourselves are overloaded and overwhelmed with our own TOO BIG feelings (and big life transitions of our own) to handle, with a baboon constantly bashing that big red fire alarm in *our* brains, too.

We cannot help our children to regulate their emotions when our own are running riot. This chapter, I think, is one of the most important – because it focuses on YOU.

Let's look, then, at how we might bring OURSELVES back to balance, and how we might find ways to fill our own 'emotional cup' without feeling guilty or selfish in doing so. When we can do this for ourselves, so we can give our children the best of US.

Where to begin? Let's start with the fundamentals.

Sleep

I'll begin by prescribing the medicine of sleep. The best gift I can give to you in this regard is to recommend the work of leading neuroscientist Professor Matthew Walker from the University of California, author of *Why We Sleep*, and Dr Ron Ehrlich, a dentist and health advocate who wrote *A Life Less Stressed: The Five*

Pillars of Health and Wellness. An online summary of their work concludes thus:

'Sleep is your in-built non-negotiable life-support system.'

It is THAT simple and, to be honest, THAT critical.

We simply cannot be the parent we want to be without it. And, yes, I know in the early weeks and months of having a baby it's nigh on impossible – I've been there! The great (always well-intentioned) advice is to 'sleep when the baby does' or 'go to bed when your children do'. But, dear Lord, how I wish we all could. Without two sets of grandparents, parents, cousins, aunts and uncles around to help out, I am not sure how any of us manage to do that, frankly. It's where we are reminded once again about the power of the extended family and a community network that recognises how much support parents need in these early years. And we ALL need support if we are not to run ourselves into the ground! So, we start by accepting SLEEP is the number-one priority, because it will help us to live our lives as parents in multi-colour, rather than a deeper shade of grey. We can then work backwards from there by asking ourselves, 'Okay, so in that case how can I ensure I get as much sleep as I can?'

> ***Brain Box*** 'If there is one thing I tell people, it's to go to bed and to wake up at the same time every day, no matter what. I take my sleep incredibly seriously because I have seen the evidence. Once you know that after just one night of only four or five hours' sleep, your natural killer cells – the ones that attack the cancer cells that appear in your body every day – drop by 70 per cent, or that a lack of sleep is ➡

linked to cancer of the bowel, prostate and breast, or even just that the World Health Organization has classed any form of night-time shift work as a probable carcinogen, how could you do anything else?'

Professor Matthew Walker, neuroscientist

Tough talk from the Prof, but I have included it here, honestly, to scare myself as much as you. I don't mean to alarm anyone, but I think we need a few home truths in this regard, as I can see how we have become a society where sleep is easily compromised, so from now on shall we make it our priority?! I do really include myself in that, because if I have learned one thing, it is that everything gets done so much easier when I am not running on empty. It is often difficult (sometimes impossible, again speaking from experience) to get everything done in the day that we need to do, but we need to do it. We compromise ourselves and our children if we don't.

Parenting with passion and understanding is so much easier when we are not tired! During quality sleep, the body and mind recharge, the brain puts the day's events in order and the physical systems within us have the chance to rest and recuperate, such as rebalancing the hormones. As Professor Walker and others have established, prolonged lack of quality sleep can lead to serious medical conditions, such as heart disease, diabetes and shorter life spans, it can also fuel low moods and depression, and lead to us putting on weight, too.

We are also more likely to operate with our ancient lizard and baboon brains when we are sleep-deprived; survival comes first, so we are more 'on edge'.

Our children and our own health depends on us getting enough sleep.

But how do we achieve the ultimate sleep as a time-poor parent?

Well, let's start with boundaries: prioritising ourselves and our eight hours of sleep above all else. Boundaries are important, whether they be with our partners who might be night owls and want to stay up late or the boss who expects us to answer their emails at 11 o'clock at night.

My sleep Holy Grail looks like this:

- At 8pm start winding down – no screens, only books, notepad by the bed for last minute to-do items.
- Write a 'five things to do tomorrow' list. It helps me to get everything out of my head, confident that I will now get these things done and can 'set them aside' as it were.
- At 9pm – in bed in a clean environment, clear of clutter and with black-out blinds.
- Between 5 and 6am – natural waking time, then tackle the most difficult items on my to-do list first!
- Maybe even get TONS OF STUFF done before the kids get up (if I'm lucky!).

You will, at least, spend the rest of the day feeling like you are ahead of the game rather than battling from behind.

I call this the Holy Grail because sleep is still my work in progress! When I try to do and be all things – mother, wife, journalist, author – sleep is often sacrificed, but after reading Matthew Walker's book, I have made it a priority now. He says we have come to think of getting enough sleep as selfish, but it's really the highest form of self-care.

Obviously, we are all different and have very varied personal circumstances, so find what works for you – just make sure you are getting enough sleep. It's not a nice extra to have – it's a necessity. SLEEP IS VITAL to you being the parent you want to be.

We can also use the word **SLEEP** as an acronym when considering the other elements of our lives that will help us to parent in balance, with emotional regulation and a 'full cup'. If **S** is for **SLEEP**, so **L** stands for **LOVE**. By this I mean the love and care you have for yourself.

Love is being kind to yourself, especially in the moments when you think you are failing as a parent – you know, those moments when you wonder why everyone else seems to find it easier than you do or have kids who actually listen.

Consider these snippets of conversations from parents I have spoken to recently:

'I feel guilty ALL the time.'

'I think I am a sh*t parent. I can't seem to get anything right.'

'Everyone else seems to have a much easier time of it – what am I doing wrong?'

'If I hear, "Mummy, come wipe my bottom," or "Mummy, come play with me," one more time . . .'

In the past, living in a community culture we would have had someone come give us a hug, to hold us in these moments and ask us how could they help or pass down their wisdoms and reassure us that they went through this, too. When we feel loved, we can in turn love. Without elders around us, we must learn to prioritise and strengthen our own internal 'support system'. With some all-important self-care.

> *Brain Box*
>
> 'Self-care for parents is so important! It can sound like a luxury, and it can certainly feel that way! When you are trying to raise children, hold down a job, manage a house, keep up relationships with family and friends ... where is there time for self-care? It is easy for that to get lost. But it's really important it doesn't. Here's why ... self-care is what lets you stay patient and emotionally regulated. Your child needs emotional stability from you, because they need help with their own emotions. It is hard to be up to the task of staying calm in the face of others' emotional needs, especially when your own reserves are depleted. So taking care of your emotional and mental health should not be last on your list. You need to take care of yourself in order to be emotionally present for your child.'
>
> Dr Suzanne Zeedyk, infant psychologist

When we give ourselves permission to be what I call 'selflessly selfish', we not only serve ourselves, but we serve our children, too.

I have learned to take 20 minutes a day (it has taken me until my children are six and eight to really feel comfortable doing it) in being 'selfish' (that's my perception, not a judgement), in taking time out for me, as I realise now just how important it is to have that headspace.

Find activities that work for you, whether it is a warm bath (science shows us it really is great for the release of anti-anxiety chemicals), or listening to a podcast or audio book. If you have a partner or friend who is able to care for your children while you take a walk, then do get outside if you can – it's so good for the soul. I can be found in the summer with my shoes off, barefoot, back against the bark of a tree, feeling the grass against the soles of my feet – it's very grounding to do that and it takes five minutes. When you prioritise yourself, even for just 20 minutes a day, you will be modelling something very powerful to your children: that self-care counts.

Getting back to the **SLEEP** acronym,

E stands for Eating . . .
What we eat has a direct and significant impact on our mood and, of course, our health. Nutritionist Kim Pearson says, 'Making healthy eating a priority for yourself also sets an important example to your children.' She advises:

- Find meals that are easy to throw together, taste good and are satisfying.
- Aim to structure meals around a source of protein (such as free-range eggs, seafood, fish, organic meat, tofu or tempeh), plenty of non-starchy vegetables or salad and a moderate portion of healthy fats (think olive oil, coconut oil, avocado, nuts and seeds).
- Batch cooking might sound like a lot of effort, but it doesn't have to be, and having a freezer full of pre-prepared, healthy meals to defrost is a godsend when time is short.
- Keeping your sugar intake to a minimum is one of the best things you can do for your and your children's health.

- It's not about never having treats; treats can absolutely form part of a healthy diet as long as they are eaten mindfully and don't end up becoming a daily habit.
- Lack of sleep has an impact on our hunger and satiety hormones, making us feel hungrier and less satisfied by the food we do eat (likewise, more naps = less nibbling).
- When we are tired, we are more likely to reach for sugary foods and those based on starchy carbohydrates (like pasta, pizza, toast, and so on).

E also stands for Exercise . . .

That is any exercise that works for you is good: it might be walking, running, swimming, cycling, bouncing. (I bought a tiny trampoline, a rebounder, this year. It folds up small, but when I need to release my own physical 'stress', boy, does it feel good to put on some headphones and bounce around for ten minutes!) Again, we are all different, so you might prefer Pilates, yoga, climbing, football – anything that calms you down, gets you out and makes you feel good. Remember, Dr Bruce Perry's research that showed how anything we do that is repetitive and rhythmic can have a hugely healing impact on our bodies and brains? I realise now why I enjoyed dancing so much on *Strictly*: there was an enormous sense of joy and well-being when I moved to music. It doesn't matter how good (or bad) we might perceive ourselves to be, if we can move in the moment to something that stimulates us, we tap into our 'inner medicine cabinet', as the scientist Uvnas Moberg calls it, with the release of oxytocin, a 'natural healing nectar' that serves as such an excellent antidote to the stress we might experience today.

I used to think of healthy food as dull, and exercise as something that needed to be endured. Now I have a very different mindset: I love cooking, and with exercise I have had more fun (and better results!) bounding around to 'shake and shimmy' out my natural stress response – in the same way I do with my children – and it's changed my attitude entirely.

P stands for PARTNERS, PEOPLE AND PLAY!

Being with warm, empathetic people can change our mood! When we are surrounded by like-minded others, it serves to lower our stress levels and help us to 'emotionally regulate'. Nadine Burke Harris points out in her book, *The Deepest Well*, that healthy relationships are a key part of healing and thriving. She discovered that caring, supportive relationships can mitigate and even prevent the lasting effects of stress in our children, and in ourselves, too. There is healing in human connection.

Parenting can take a toll on relationships; it can expose cracks that can become chasms, requiring great stoicism and connectedness on our part to parent together when often we might feel like we are pulling apart. Again, having community support can help to support us in times when we might feel that we are floundering, as does sharing our experience with emotionally available friends, not fearing judgement, or speaking to professionals, charities or relatives. Very often the tensions we experience, especially in the early years of having children, might well pass, but having help ... helps. Equally, if it doesn't, then seeking professional support can be more beneficial for you and for your children in the long run, too. I list some resources in the back of this book, and include suggestions of ways to find and build a network of parents/professionals in the area that you live. Online communities can be very supportive, too. That said, I personally feel that there is perhaps more power in actually meeting in person: the touch of someone's hand on ours if we are in pain is so much more powerful than in the virtual world. We are social beings, pack animals, and as paediatric registrar Dr Guddi Singh said at the start of Chapter 13, 'hugs can change the world'!

Without the benefit or luxury now of living in extended families, I cannot emphasise enough how important it is to feel able to reach out if you do need support to 'find your tribe'. And we will all need support . . . even the toughest among us.

 ## Man-ouevres with Mike

'No one would get through military training without camaraderie. During particularly tough times when we were on arduous treks or yomps there would be a fair amount of complaining, albeit humorous. No matter how bad it got, or how cold, wet and miserable the environment was, no matter how grave the danger, a bit of dark banter would get us through. If the banter or complaining stopped, then that was a worry because it meant someone could be shutting down, switching off. When we were somewhere that was seriously cold, that could mean hypothermia was potentially kicking in. We NEED each other in these moments. That goes for parents, too.'

Mike adds: 'Here's another other lesson from the Marines that I still use to help me parent: we used to say that no matter how cold/ hot/wet/hungry/bitten by insects/covered in blisters you are, it can all be taken away by a hot shower, a meal and a good night's sleep. I would tell myself that a lot when my kids were young (I still do!).'

Looking after ourselves, being around like-minded others, carving ourselves 20 minutes a day for some all-important headspace (what I think of allowing our minds to 'play!') is crucial if we are to have the headspace for our children and their care. Play for adults, in my mind, extends to things like meditation, acupuncture, massage, yoga and breathing exercises, which can all help stimulate our own anti-anxiety chemicals and that all-important love drug, the hormone oxytocin. Play, for me, means taking time out to remember who we are as people, not just mums or dads, but the person we have become.

TOOL KIT TIP

Butterfly hugs and hand breathing

What is the best way to calm our own baboon and lizard when we are home alone and the children are running us ragged? Butterfly hugs and hand breathing are two tools we can carry around with us all the time and are entirely free of charge.

Butterfly hugs

The butterfly hug was developed by Lucina Artigas, a therapist who worked with children in the aftermath of a natural disaster in Mexico City in 1998. It can be very effective in daily life, too. It works by stimulating both sides of the brain in what is called 'self-administered bilateral stimulation'. I find it very effective for calming and grounding us. The principle is easy enough:

- Start by crossing your arms over your chest so that the tip of the middle finger from each hand is placed below your collarbone. Your hands must be as vertical as possible, so that your fingers point towards the neck and not towards the arms. Raise your elbows to create the butterfly wings. Your eyes can be closed, or partially closed, looking towards the tip of your nose.

- Next, you slowly tap your hands on your chest, alternating left and right. Breathe slowly and deeply in through your nose and exhale through your nose until you start to feel some relief.

I find myself coming back to 'calm' very quickly when I do this very gentle, simple exercise. Allow your thoughts to run freely, just letting the thoughts around sounds, smells and physical sensations simply float in and away without judgement.

The butterfly hug can be done anywhere you feel comfortable: standing, sitting in a chair or lying down, with your eyes open or closed. For more details and a demonstration you can research this in more detail online (see page 297).

Next we have . . .

Hand Breathing

This is a very simple but effective technique that is used widely by therapists and in schools, too.

- Stretch your hand out like a star in front of you. Using the index finger of your other hand, begin to trace up and down each finger, starting from the thumb and drawing your finger up and down each, breathing deeply as you go.
- Breathe in through your nose as you trace up the finger, then out through your mouth as you bring the finger back down. Keep going until you have finished tracing your hand.

I find this such an excellent way to find calm, especially if I am facing something particularly difficult emotionally, either in my counselling training or when I am at home and there is a lot to juggle. I have learned to use my breath a lot; if I am under pressure, I simply breathe in through my nose and let the breath out through pursed lips. This is just how I do it – there are many different methods and good people advising on brilliant breathing techniques (see pages 297 and 301.).

We can also teach our children these techniques; they will stand you and them in very good stead, whatever the circumstances.

* * *

It takes a village to raise a child

Nelson Mandela said, 'There can be no keener revelation of a society's soul than the way it treats its children.' And it's true, we are a collective – or at least should be – when it comes to raising our families. We are so much stronger when we can pull together, and support each other, both nationally, and in our own communities and friendship groups.

In 2020, the Royal Foundation (see page 299) launched a landmark survey on the under-fives and gave people across the UK an opportunity to provide their view on raising the next generation. The research looked at how difficult experiences in early childhood are often the root cause of key social challenges such as poor mental health, family breakdown, addiction and homelessness. The Duchess of Cambridge unveiled the findings of what became the biggest ever UK study on families in society and it found, among other things, that the reality of modern life made it very hard for parents to prioritise their well-being. Only 10 per cent of parents who took part in the survey mentioned taking the time to look after their own well-being, for example, when asked how they had prepared for the arrival of their baby. Some 70 per cent of parents said they felt judged by others and, among these, nearly half felt it negatively impacted their mental health. The survey identified a high incidence of parental loneliness, with many parents saying they felt uncomfortable seeking help for how they are feeling.

Covid-19 and some of the national policies to deal with it – in the form of lockdowns and school closures – served to increase the pressure on families and children's mental health in general. In challenging times, when we are increasingly time-poor and emotionally depleted, it has never been more important to find solace in the company of others, even for just a few minutes in the day, something to ensure we are reminded and reassured we are not alone.

I have personally found great comfort in the company of 'good women', whether they are my sisters, Claire and Amy, my friends, my school mums, neighbours or work colleagues. I really value them and their advice, finding solace in being able to offload and chat, to laugh at the 'small silly stuff', our parenting 'fails' and supporting each other with pick-ups or play dates, just to share experiences and normalise how we feel. I appreciate and value the men in my life, too; they often bring a different perspective and regularly floor me with their compassion and kindness, especially in their care for their children. I know from my conversations with fathers that they can often feel they are running to catch up when it comes to parenting. And I strongly feel they also need our support, to hear practical advice from people they can relate to, and to know they don't have to go through this alone.

Parent ponders: René, now dad to two grown-up children, was bereaved when they were very young

'Nothing is best done alone any more, especially parenting. What sup-port do you have? I had part of my life bringing up my son alone, then with my wife during my daughter's younger years, then I lost my wife and I was on my own again. So, I know the benefit of two of you: it is so much more powerful. There were some things I was brilliant at, and some things my wife was brilliant at – I was the doer, the taxi, I banged the nails in, I would run to the shops, taking them to football and taking them swimming; she was the listener.

'After she passed away, I remember going to the Gingerbread Club where it was all mothers and I was the only father. I remember the cool-ness of the reception and they were convinced that I had just turned up in the wrong place; they weren't hostile, but it certainly wasn't warm, and it took three or four times turning up before that changed. But I didn't let that stop me – I thought: I am going to go again, I want the relationships, I want the bonding, I want the learning, I want the network. I still remember feeling odd turning up to dinner parties on my own, without a partner. There was no allowance for that fact. But thankfully there were girlfriends, there were neighbours, there were other parents that I could talk to and I would invite parents to come round with their kids, because it helped me just to be in an environment where we all had kids.

You want to be a role-model parent and I hope that there is someone around, maybe a couple that you can learn from, who mentor you, if you like. It's more than just shared wisdom: you've got the safety, the connection, the camaraderie.'

Man-ouevres with Mike

'I liken the first few weeks of fatherhood to wandering around in a darkened room full of rakes. Some days it will seem as if you are treading on every single one. It can be difficult to adjust to our new role having a "walk-on part", where once we were the lead. Often, we are left wondering what on earth to do and how best to help. I can honestly say that as an older father, with no living parents, I did not receive one bit of guidance or useful advice from anyone other than "it's tougher than you think" and "trust your instincts". But I'm not sure that it was that instinctive and it can leave you open to all sorts of mistakes. I've actually had way more guidance with our new puppy than for a new baby.

'Whether you are parenting alone or in a partnership, whether you are the biological father or not, I believe strongly in the role we fathers play in our children's lives. I think sometimes we may feel the lesser qualified (or maybe that was just me?!), but I now see what a crucial role we play in raising our children. They need us just as much, and, frankly, I think we need them, too. Fatherhood is an enriching life experience and one I am so grateful for. To quote Abraham Lincoln, "No man stands so tall as when he stoops to help a child." I applaud René for his determination and tenacity, especially when facing his own grief and loss. As his example demonstrates, don't be afraid to ask questions – we all start somewhere and in my book there are no "stupid" questions. Trust yourself, Google doesn't always know best, pull together as a team and know that what you do WILL make a difference.'

I found the most enlightening, comforting conversations about parenting are the ones I have with other parents when we are really honest about how we feel and what we might be struggling with, or the questions we really want to ask but have been too afraid to. It is in these moments we might realise our children are all the same. There is nothing wrong with them, just as there is nothing wrong with us as parents – we might just be at a different stage of a challenge. And this is where *community* can bring such comfort. Life can often feel overwhelming and difficult, with hardship and heartache. But the load can be lessened when we are able to share our experience with others, in fact, as humans once naturally did.

Brain Box

'Our brain evolved over hundreds of thousands of generations in small hunter-gatherer bands where a complex, interactive, dynamic, socio-emotional environment provided the experiences for the developing child. In a group of 150, there were three or more adult caregiving adults for every dependent child under age six. Children grew up in the presence of the elderly, siblings, adults — related and not. There was a more continuous exposure and wider variety of socio-emotional interactions. The effect of modern lifestyle, communications, technology and economies is that we are now raising children in environments that are very different from the rich social context for which our brains are most suited.'

Kate Stanley and Dr Nathaniel Kendall-Taylor,
FrameWorks Institute
Professor Peter Fonagy, Anna Freud Centre for Children and Families

---

I hope society can come together to focus on these issues and on the most crucial years of our children's lives, from conception through to five years old, and focus on us as parents, too, because we need all the help and support we can get. It really is too crucial for future generations not to do so.

In the words of the African proverb, 'It takes a village to raise a child.'

* * *

How were you parented?

It's good to consider what wisdoms we had passed down to us by our parents or others. The child clinical psychologist Oliver James asserts that, 'we either rebel against the way we were parented or follow that form of parenting precisely'. I think it's healthy when we are able to honestly reflect and consider how we ourselves were parented. We might ask ourselves what do we remember as the best things ... and the worst? What would we wish to repeat with our own children and what would we not? My hope is that you are able to be curious about what made *you* feel safe and happy as a child, keeping the best bits of your experience and consider being open to changing the rest that you didn't enjoy. (There are lots of resources at the back of the book with reference to this topic.) If it feels a little difficult for you to practise self-care or reflect on your own experience as a child in that regard, having therapy can be a great place to start, because a good therapist can help you to 're-parent' your own inner child. This is obviously a whole other book in itself (and one I would love to write!) but for now it might be a consideration if you think you need a bit of support in this department (see Resources for how to find one that is right for you), but there is a lot you can do for yourself, too. In spite of all the traumas and worries in the world, when we have the right people around us we can come through. When we feel supported and heard ourselves, so we can find the space to give of ourselves to our children, too. As they say on planes, 'put your own oxygen mask on before helping anyone else'.

Western parenting can tend to be terribly critical and, as a society, we can be very judgemental – or at least we can FEEL we are being judged. So, let's turn the tables on that and start viewing ourselves with more compassion. We are doing the very best we can to make our children happy.

And that is ENOUGH.

Parent ponders: René

'As a single father it took me a long time to realise that I didn't need to play to anyone's rules but my own. At times I felt that feeling of being the outsider, I felt guilt, I felt inadequate, but you should never feel this when you are trying to do your best as a parent.'

We serve ourselves and our children when we trust precisely that. When we can all sit with the knowledge that:

- No parent is perfect.
- There is always an opportunity to start over – tomorrow is a new day.
- If we get it right even just some of the time, it can be enough. Starting with small steps we can make big changes!
- Whatever has gone before, has gone before. There is always room for repair, both in ourselves and in the relationship we have with our children.

When I embarked on the journey of writing this book, the aim was to share what I had learned about these early years of our children's lives: that what we experience when we are very young will shape the adult we become. We know that what we do as parents in the first five years of our children's lives will be pivotal to their future health and happiness. We know we can help our children best when we are able to see the world through their eyes. I hope that in telling the story of the lizard, the baboon and the wise owl, it might help you to see your children as I have been able to see mine.

Our children are full of brilliant, beautiful potential, and to help them fulfil it all we need to do is *see* them and *hear* them, to understand how they're driven by ancient brains and really *big* emotions. When we respond to them with compassion and understanding, we can rest assured that all our children really need is us, our presence, however imperfect we might sometimes feel.

It starts with *us*, it starts now. It starts when we can – hand on heart – believe that *there really is no such thing as 'naughty'*.

Bibliography

The websites in this list are those accessed by the author for research purposes – their inclusion does not indicate that the author endorses them.

CHAPTER 1

Gerhardt, S., *Why Love Matters*, Routledge (2004).

Fonagy, P., 'A deeper dive into the science of early childhood and the key insights that built today's knowledge (briefing papers); Gogtay, N. and Giedd, J. N., et al., 'Dynamic mapping of human cortical development during childhood through early adulthood', *Proc Natl Acad Sci USA* (2004): 101(21), 8174–79; Dennis, E. L. and Jahanshad N., et al., 'Development of brain structural connectivity between ages 12 and 30: a 4-Tesla diffusion imaging study in 439 adolescents and adults', *Neuroimage* (2013): 64, 671–84; Zielinski, B. A., Gennatas, E. D., Zhou, J., Seeley, W.W., 'Network-level structural covariance in the developing brain', *Proc Natl Acad Sci USA* (2010): 107(42), 18191–96.

Jenny Smith: midwife and founder of jentlechildbirth.co.uk and birthcontinua.com.

van der Kolk, B. A., *The Body Keeps the Score: Brain, Mind and Body in the Healing of Trauma*, Penguin (2015).

The British psychiatrist John Bowlby defined attachment as

a 'lasting psychological connectedness between human beings'. For more information, visit: thebowlbycentre.org.uk/about-the-bowlby-centre/.

Dr Allan Schore's website and more information on his work can be found at: www.allanschore.com.

CHAPTER 2

Sunderland, M., *The Science of Parenting*, DK (2016).

Zeedyk, S., *Sabre Tooth Tigers and Teddy Bears: The connected baby guide to attachment* (2014), suzannezeedyk.com/books-dvds-ecourses-suzanne-zeedyk/.

Burke Harris, N., *The Deepest Well: Healing the Long-term Effects of Childhood Adversity*, Bluebird (2018).

National Scientific Council on the Developing Child (2005/2014), 'Excessive Stress Disrupts the Architecture of the Developing Brain: Working Paper No. 3' (updated edition). Retrieved from www.developingchild.harvard.edu; Also see, developingchild.harvard.edu/science/key-concepts/toxic-stress/.

Dawson, G., et al., 'The role of early experience in shaping behavioural and brain development and its implications for social policy', *Developmental Psychology* (autumn 2000): 12(4), 695–712.

Gunnar, M. R., 'Studies of the human infants adrenocortical response to potentially stressful events', *New Directions for Child Development* (Fall 1989): 3–18.

CHAPTER 3

Anna Freud National Centre for Children and Families: www.annafreud.org.

Margaret Heffernan: for more information visit: www.mheffernan.com/index.php.

Trauma Informed Schools: www.traumainformedschools.co.uk.

The Harvard Center on the Developing Child: developingchild. harvard.edu.

CHAPTER 4

Dr Paul Ekman: for more information visit www.paulekman. com.

Plutchik, R., *The Emotions*, University Press of America (1991 revised edition).

Zeedyk, S., *Sabre Tooth Tigers and Teddy Bears: The connected baby guide to attachment* (2014), suzannezeedyk.com/ books-dvds-ecourses-suzanne-zeedyk/.

Still face experiment: developed by Dr Ed Tronick in the 1970s, the 'still face' experiment offers insight into how a parent's reactions can affect the emotional development of a baby, and underlines the need for 'connection' from very early in life: www.gottman.com/blog/ research-still-face-experiment/.

On still face, also see www.ncbi.nlm.nih.gov/pmc/articles/ PMC3289403/; https://dennis-tiwary.com/wp-content/uploads/2015/01/ Gulyayeva-et-al-Still-Face-poster-from-APS-2016-conference. pdf; Dennis-tiwary.com; and www.childforum.com/images/stories/2013_Blaiklock_published. pdf.

Sunderland, M., *The Science of Parenting*, DK (2016).

CHAPTER 5

Sunderland, M., *The Science of Parenting*, DK (2016).

Child Trauma Academy: for more information visit www. childtrauma.org.

Dr Bruce Perry: for more information on Dr Perry's work, visit www.bdperry.com and see his many books, including *The Boy Who Was Raised as a Dog*, Basic Books (2017).

Schacter, D., *Searching for Memory: The Brain, the Mind and the Past*, Basic Books (1997).

Perry, B., *Splintered Reflections: Images of the Body in Trauma*, Jean Goodwin, Reina Attias (eds), Basic Books (1999).

James, O., *How to Develop Emotional Health*, Macmillan (2014).

Middlemiss, W. 1., Granger, D. A., Goldberg, W. A. and Nathans L., 'A synchrony of mother-infant hypothalamic-pituitary-adrenal axis activity following extinction of infant crying responses induced during the transition to sleep', *Early Hum Dev.* (Apr. 2012), 88(4): 227–32. doi: 10.1016/j.earlhumdev.2011.08.010. Epub 2011 Sep 23.

Maté, G., 'Why I No Longer Believe Babies Should Cry Themselves to Sleep', on Gabor Maté's official website, drgabormate.com/no-longer-believe-babies-cry-sleep/; see also Maté, G., *When The Body Says No: The Cost of Hidden Stress*, Vermilion (2019).

CHAPTER 6

Levine, P., '*Waking the Tiger: Healing Trauma: The Innate Capacity to Transform Overwhelming Experiences*', North Atlantic Books (2011).

CHAPTER 8

Dr Gabor Maté: for more information see his website drgabormate.com.

John Bowlby: for more information, visit thebowlbycentre.org.uk.

CHAPTER 9

Rozin, P. and Royzman, E. B., 'Negativity Bias, Negativity Dominance, and Contagion', *Personality and Social Psychology Review* (2001), 5(4): 296–320.

CHAPTER 10

Anna Freud National Centre for Children and Families: www. annafreud.org.

Sigman, A., *Remotely Controlled: How television is damaging our lives*, Vermilion (2007); Sigman, A., 'Screen Dependency Disorders: a new challenge for child neurology', *Journal of the International Child Neurology Association* (April 2017). See also: 'Children under five should spend less than an hour a day in front of the TV: Doctors say electronic screens damage youngsters' sleep and fitness', *Daily Mail*, 13 November, 2016.

The American Academy of Pediatrics can be found at: www. aap.org.

CHAPTER 11

developingchild.harvard.edu/science/key-concepts/ brain-architecture/.

NSPCC: www.nspcc.org.uk.

Place2Be: www.place2be.org.uk.

CHAPTER 12

Age gap/sibling rivalry research: there are two types of research, physical and mental. For more information on physical health see the Weston A. Price Foundation website, westonaprice.org; for more information on mental well-being see Laura Markham talking about this subject at www.ahaparenting.com/ask-the-doctor-1/ what-is-the-best-age-spacing-between-siblings.

Biddulph, S., *Raising Boys*, HarperNonFiction (2018); see also stevebiddulph.com and 'Kids in lockdown: why it's much harder for boys', Steve Biddulph writing in *The Times*, 17 April, 2020.

Shumaker, H., *It's OK Not to Share*, Tarcher (2012); see also heatherschumaker.com.

Laura Markham: *Calm Parents, Happy Siblings: The Secrets of Stress-free Parenting*, Vermilion (2015), and *Peaceful Parent, Happy Kids*, Perigree Books (2014); also see ahaparenting. com.

Fabre, A. and Mazlish, E., *Siblings Without Rivalry*, Piccadilly Press (1999).

Eisenberg, N., 'Eight Tips to Developing Caring Kids', in *Good Things To Do: Expert Suggestions for Fostering Goodness in Kids*, Portland, David Streight (ed.) (2009).

CHAPTER 13

Pereira Gray, D., Dean, D., Dineen, M. and Dean, P., 'Science versus society: is childcare for the under threes a taboo subject?', *Epigenomics*, Future Medicine Ltd (2020).

O' Sullivan, J., *The A to Z of Early Years: Politics, Pedagogy and Plain Speaking*, Sage Publications (2020).

The London Early Years Foundation: leyf.org.uk.

CHAPTER 14

Walker, M., *Why We Sleep: The New Science of Sleep and Dreams*, Penguin (2018).

Ehrlich, R., *A Life Less Stressed: The Five Pillars of Health and Wellness*, Scribe UK (2018).

Uvnas Moberg, Kerstin: for more information on oxytocin, visit www.kerstinuvnasmoberg.com

Uvnas Moberg, K., and Odent, M., *The Oxytocin Factor: Tapping the Hormone of Calm, Love, and Healing*, Pinter & Martin Ltd (2011); Uvnas Moberg, K., *The Hormone of Closeness: The Role of Oxytocin in Relationships*, Pinter & Martin Ltd (2013); and Uvnas Moberg, K., *Oxytocin: The Biological Guide to Motherhood*, Praeclarus Press (2016).

Burke Harris, N., *The Deepest Well: Healing the Long-Term Effects of Childhood Adversity*, Bluebird (2018).

Butterfly hug: for more information see www.researchgate.net/publication/340280320_The_EMDR_Therapy_Butterfly_Hug_Method_for_Self-Administer_Bilateral_Stimulation/.

Hand breathing: for more information see childhood101.com/take-5-breathing-exercise/.

The Royal Foundation: royalfoundation.com/5-big-questions/.

James, O., *How to Develop Emotional Health*, Macmillan (2014).

Resources

The following organisations have fantastic websites that are a goldmine of information and offer an enormous source of expert opinion and findings:

Action for Children, www.actionforchildren.org.uk/
Advance (Advocacy and Non Violence Community
  Education) Charity (domestic violence; age 5 to 18), www.
  advancecharity.org.uk/
Barnardo's (offers Helpline – including one specifically for
  minorities), www.barnardos.org.uk
Child Bereavement UK, www.childbereavementuk.org/
Childline, www.childline.org.uk/
Children First – Scotland, www.children1st.org.uk/
The Children's Society, www.childrenssociety.org.uk/
Mentally Healthy Schools, www.mentallyhealthyschools.
  org.uk/
Mind, www.mind.org.uk/information-support/
  for-children-and-young-people/
Royal Foundation, royalfoundation.com/programme/early-
  years/
SAMARITANS (Helpline open to under 18s), www.samaritans.
  org/
UK Trauma Council, uktraumacouncil.org

Voice collective (support for children and young people who hear voices, see visions or have other unusual sensory experiences), www.voicecollective.co.uk/

WATCH – What about the children (0–3 years), www.whataboutthechildren.org.uk/

Winston's Wish, www.winstonswish.org/

Anna Freud National Centre for Children and Families, www.annafreud.org

NSPCC, www.nspcc.org.uk

Place2Be is an incredible organisation and I urge you to visit www.place2be.org.uk

Maudsley Foundation, maudsleycharity.org

The American Academy of Pediatrics, www.aap.org

Employers' Initiative on Domestic Abuse, www.eida.org.uk

Heads Together Foundation, royalfoundation.com

Mind, www.mind.org.uk

Cruse Bereavement, www.cruse.org.uk

Epione Training, www.epione-training.com

Home-Start UK, www.home-start.org.uk

Laura Henry Consultancy, www.laurahenryconsultancy.com

ACE Aware Nation, aceawarescotland.com

70/30 Campaign, www.70-30.org.uk

Anxiety UK, www.anxietyuk.org.uk

BACP.co.uk is an excellent resource for finding a therapist

Sane, www.sane.org.uk

Mental Health Foundation, www.mentalhealth.org.uk

Time to Change, www.time-to-change.org.uk

Best Beginnings, www.bestbeginnings.org.uk

Young Minds, youngminds.org.uk

Chance UK, www.chanceuk.com

Children In Need, www.bbcchildreninneed.co.uk

Violence Reduction Units – Scotland/London, www.svru.co.uk

NVR Northampton, www.nvrnorthampton.co.uk

Women's Aid, www.womensaid.org.uk
Beacon House, beaconhouse.org.uk
www.vroom.org
breathpod.me
Familylives.org.uk
Familyequality.org
Joseph Rowntree Organisation, www.jrf.org.uk
Aimh.uk
mothersathomematter.com
Parentsasfirstteachers.org
Wavetrust.org
fivetothrive.org.uk
childmentalhealth.org
brainwave.org.nz

Acknowledgements

To everyone who helped to bring this dream to reality – thank you

To everyone at Piatkus, Little, Brown: to Zoe, Jillian, Clara, Aimee, Sarah, Andy and the entire team for going the extra mile and for 'getting it' from the get-go.

Amanda Bannister at Bannister Creative for being brilliantly astute, always available and always oh, so impeccably attired.

Bev James, Tom Wright and the team at Bev James Management, what a pleasure it has been, I am looking forward to what is to come!

Sarah, Leonie, Malcolm and all those at the BBC who enabled me to take the time.

Korda Ace, for the divine illustrations. You have a wonderful talent and it has been such a joy – thank you for bringing my 'babies' to life!

To Dave's dad ... who may at some points have wished he had never picked up the phone, but whose hand-holding and faith in me encouraged me to get this book over the line. To Yoda in disguise ... Mart, thank you!

Benny and Robbie for your friendship, wisdom and unwavering support. Thank you being such a force for good in the world of children's mental health.

Peter, you once charged me with writing a book to communicate the science. Thank you for having the faith in me to do so, for your feedback throughout and for your endorsement of the result. Thank you for all that you do for children and families everywhere.

Bruce, thank you for the interviews, your feedback and for writing the book *The Boy Who Was Raised as a Dog*, where, more than a decade ago, you first drew my attention to the reality of life for maltreated children.

Suzanne, your energy and spirit never cease to buoy my work. My love and thanks for all that you do – and for the detailed feedback you so generously gave.

Margot and Gabor, thank you for writing the books that have inspired and spurred me on.

A very special thank you to those who read initial drafts and for giving so generously of your time and expertise in feedback when you were already working at capacity:

Dr Dickon Bevington, Consultant in Child and Adolescent Psychiatry in the NHS

Susan Cooke, Head of Research NSPCC

Diana Dean, Research Director, WATCH

Professor Peter Fonagy OBE, National Clinical Advisor to NHS England on Children and Young People's Mental Health, Chief Executive of the Anna Freud Centre, London

Professor Eamon McCrory, Professor of Developmental Neuroscience and Psychopathology, Co-Founder of the UK Trauma Council and a Director at the Anna Freud Centre

Dr Bruce Perry, MD, PhD, Principal of the Neurosequential Network, Senior Fellow of The Child Trauma Academy

Dr Suzanne Zeedyk, Infant Psychologist, Research Scientist, Founder of *Connected Baby*.

Many thanks to Duncan Wardle, former Head of Innovation and Creativity at Disney, for the 'cardboard box' inspiration! www.duncanwardle.com

With special thanks for their support and contributions to this book. In alphabetical order:

Dr Bruce Clark, Consultant Child and Adolescent Psychiatrist, Clinical Director for child and adolescent mental health service at the Maudsley Hospital

Julie Harmieson, Co-Director of Trauma Informed Schools UK

Prof Sir Denis Pereira Gray OBE, FRCP, FRCGP, FMedSci

Dr Gabor Maté, Physician, Addiction Expert and Author

June O'Sullivan MBE, Chief Executive London Early Years Foundation

Dr Matthew Patrick former Chief Executive of South London and Maudsley NHS Foundation Trust

Place2Be Founder and President, Dame Benita Refson DBE and The Hon Robert A. Rayne

Dr Dan Siegel, Clinical Professor of Psychiatry at the UCLA School of Medicine and the founding co-director of the Mindful Awareness Research Center at UCLA.

Georgia Robinson-Steele Dip.Couns, Founder Kent Well-being Hub

Catherine Roche, CEO Place2Be

Dr Margot Sunderland, Director of Education and Training at The Centre for Child Mental Health London

Sir Peter Wanless CB, Chief Executive of the NSPCC

To the organisations and charities I have been honoured and proud to work with and support for the past fifteen years and more . . . thank you for the work that you do.

Anna Freud National Centre for Children and Families

NSPCC

Place2Be

Royal Foundation

To my Place2Be gang – the most gorgeous, brilliant group of women who walked by my side as we studied during lockdown . . .

we 'played', we laughed, we did good work. Forever thanks to Georgia and Beq, who taught us so much and got me to dig deeper each time.

To Kim, Kez, Marianne, Tom, Matt and Brooke, thank you for your creative input, your spirit and beautiful energy and support.

To special friends – for being there with cups of tea, cycles (and the odd G&T), Rosie, Natalie, Susanna, Penny, Sara, Jonty and Tye, Caroline, Lisa, Andy, Becca and my Op Raleigh crew, thank you for keeping me going with eccentric chats, catch-ups and for it never feeling like more than ten minutes since I saw you last.

Special mention to Kevin Neary, James Docherty, Iain Smith, Pauline Scott, Callum Hutchison, Karyn McCluskey, John Carnochan, Prof Sir Harry Burns, Dr Christine Goodall, Dr Nadine Burke Harris, Niven Rennie and all the inspirational people working to inspire a society that is truly 'trauma-informed'.

To my fellow and oh-so-fabulous mums and dads who shared their tales of love and contributed that sparkle and magic to the book. To Rosie Nixon, Claire, Alpa Patel, Ali MacLaine and René Carayol – thank you for your honesty and integrity and for being the most incredible parents too!

To Jenny Smith – my midwife and the most beautiful human on the planet, who brought my two babies into the world. Thank you to the stars and back . . . your selflessness and talent needs to be cloned.

To Liza Elle – thank you for your wisdom, your loving dedication and for always encouraging me to find my path. There are too few words to convey how much you have taught me.

To MY mum – Mum, you are incredible. Thank you for everything; for the cups of tea and cuddles and for showing me how roast dinners can be a cure for everything! You have been incredible this past year. How wonderful to be published on your birthday. I know Daddy is looking down and cheering from the rafters. I love you both very, very much.

To Claire and Amy – mothers to eight children between you – you rock! You are mothers above and beyond. Thanks for the laughter this year and for the love we share, for the feedback on my many cover incarnations and for our husbands (hurrah!) and our children too.

To Clemency and Wilbur (and not forgetting Gatsby), thank you for being the best, most beautiful and brightest stars in my night sky. You're amazing and I love you with all my heart. Thank you for allowing me to share your stories. Thank you for inspiring me to be a better mum every single day.

Finally, to my husband Mike. To my ever-guiding light, to my sea and to the boat we both sail. You know how much I love you and I know how much you hate a public display – but here it is. Thank you for finding me. I love you. Always.

Index